JOUMANA HADDAD is ... translator, publisher and journ... Arab world's first erotic cultura... ...ch made headlines around the worl... ...ed as one of the Beirut39 authors in 2009. *I K... ...erazade: Confessions of an Angry Arab Woman* was critically acclaimed and translated into thirteen languages. She lives in Beirut with her two sons.

Praise for *I Killed Scheherazade: Confessions of an Angry Arab Woman*

'A spirited call to arms' *New York Times*

'A vivid assertion of individuality, free speech, free choice and dignity against religious bigotry, prejudice and the herd instinct both within and outside the Arab world.' *Guardian*

'Haddad is a poet who inhabits the storm.' Tahar Ben Jelloun

'In this courageous book Haddad breaks down the taboo of the silent absent Arab woman.' Elfriede Jelinek

'Haddad is a revolutionary, this book is the manifesto. Read it or be left behind.' Rabih Alameddine

'Courageous and illuminating … it opens our eyes, destroys our prejudices and is very entertaining.' Mario Vargas Llosa

'Haddad cannot be intimidated. This book is a lesson of courage for all those who fight to go beyond their own limits and chains.' Roberto Saviano

'Lifts the veil on love and sex' *Marie Claire*

ALSO BY JOUMANA HADDAD

I Killed Scheherazade: Confessions of an Angry Arab Woman

JOUMANA HADDAD

Superman is an Arab

On God, Marriage, Macho Men
and Other Disastrous Inventions

The Westbourne Press

First published 2012 by The Westbourne Press

1

© Joumana Haddad 2012

ISBN 978-1-908906-09-0

eISBN 978-1-908906-08-3

A full CIP record for this book is available from the British Library.

A full CIP record for this book is available from the Library of Congress.

Printed and bound by CPI Group (UK) Ltd, Croydon, CRO 4YY

The Westbourne Press
26 Westbourne Grove, London W2 5RH
www.westbournepress.co.uk

To my two sons,
Mounir and Ounsi.
May they grow to become less 'Supermen'
and more real 'men':
Men I can be proud of,
Men they are proud to be.

This then? This is not a book, in the ordinary sense of the word. No, this is a prolonged insult, a gob of spit, a kick in the pants to God, Man, Destiny, Time … I am going to sing for you, a little off key perhaps, but I will sing.
Henry Miller (Tropic of Cancer)

I, with a deeper instinct, choose a man who compels my strength, who makes enormous demands on me, who does not doubt my courage or my toughness, who does not believe me naive or innocent, who has the courage to treat me like a woman.
Anaïs Nin

The tragedy of machismo is that a man is never quite man enough.
Germaine Greer

Contents

Once upon a time …

Once upon a time, there was a little girl who loved to read more than anything else in the whole wide world. She read everything she could get her hands on: her father's newspapers, her mother's glossy magazines, and all the books that were stuffed in their house's big library. She even read the tiny information leaflets that come inside drug boxes, notifying users about dosage, administration and side effects. That's how she learnt, by age eight, that antacids and alcohol were not a good mix, and that 'Ranitidine may decrease the absorption of diazepam and reduce its plasma concentration': warnings which proved not to be very useful later in her life.

She read while she was having lunch (to her mother's despair); at break time in school (to her friends' disappointment); during the courses she wasn't interested in (geography is way overrated); when she was riding the bus (that's why she often missed her station and arrived late); in the shelter where she used to hide from the bombings during the civil war taking place outside (much more efficient than ear plugs) … And at night-time, when everybody else was sleeping, she would sneak a lamp light under her bed sheet and read.

Needless to say, that little girl was me.

Comic books were never available at home. First of all, they were a kind of luxury that cost too much money; or at least too much money for a modest middle-class family like mine. Secondly, they weren't 'serious' enough reads for my traditional dad, who disdained any sentence that you didn't have to read at least twice in order to fully understand. So I was mostly unaware of the existence of comics. Until one day – I must have been nine or ten – when we were visiting my aunt's house and as I was feeling increasingly excluded between three cousins (all male) and a brother who were playing 'catch me if you can', I found a stack of Superman magazines in a corner. I delved into them immediately. And what a discovery it was.

I loved Clark Kent right away. He was a timid, clumsy, honest, sweet, mild-mannered man. He was, in short, genuine. But every time he ripped open his street clothes and turned into Superman, flying away out of a window to presumably save the human race, I felt a kind of discomfort and distress. I couldn't quite put my finger on the reason why I disliked him so much, especially since he was such an admirable hero in appearance. But I couldn't help it. I was put off by the character who is 'faster than a speeding bullet and more powerful than a locomotive' and who can 'change the course of mighty rivers and bend iron with his bare hands'. I didn't see Clark Kent as a disguise for him, but the other way around. And I strongly resented Lois Lane's affection for Superman, and rejection of Kent.

Then it suddenly hit me one day, much, much later: this world (and women in it) doesn't need manufactured 'men of steel'. It needs *real* men. Real men, yes: with all their clumsiness, timidity, flaws, slips and weak spots. Real men who don't have secret identities. Real men who don't think they can see further than you, hear more accurately than you, run faster than you and worst of all, think better than you. Real men who don't need to put on blue tights and a red cape (an odd metaphor for virility) in order to feel empowered. Real men who aren't convinced they are invincible. Real men who aren't afraid to show their vulnerable sides. Real men who don't hide their true personalities from you (or from themselves). Real men who don't feel embarrassed to solicit help when they need it. Real men who are proud to be supported by you, as much as they are proud to support you. Real men who don't identify themselves with the dimensions of their penises and breadth of their chest hair. Real men who don't define themselves by their sexual performance. Real men who don't define themselves by their bank accounts. Real men who carefully listen to you instead of arrogantly trying to rescue you. Real men who don't feel mortified and castrated if every now and then they fail to have an erection. Real men who discuss what's best for both of you *with* you, instead of arrogantly saying, 'leave it up to me'. Real men who consider you a partner and not a victim/mission/trophy. Real men who share their problems and worries with you, instead of insisting on solving them by themselves. Real men who, in a nutshell, aren't shy to ask for directions, instead of pretending they know it all (frequently at the price of getting lost).

This world definitely doesn't need Supermen. Why? Well, first of all, because Superman is a fictional character. Many of you will say at this point: *Duh! What's new? Of course he is.* Well, guess what: in my world (and in certain parts of yours as well, I am sure), many think he *really* exists. But that is not the real problem. I am not talking about the 'imaginary friend/saviour' syndrome here. The real problem is that those who believe in the idea of Superman are convinced they *are* him. And act accordingly. And that is when everything goes wrong. That is when leaders become despots, bosses become slave owners, believers become terrorists and boyfriends become oppressors. All in the name of 'I know your interests better than you'. Yes, a fictional character *can* become a human calamity. And although it might seem funny at times, it is not. It is sad. And destructive. To oneself and to others.

The reality described above is the reason why I was struck by an analogy later, one that seemed quite credible to me: Superman is an *Arab*. The same split personality. The same pretentious 'I can save the day' attitude. The same macho manners. The same 'I am Good and the rest are Evil' stance. The same 'I am indestructible' delusion. There are so many of these self-appointed superheroes here, in my dear old Arab region, whether they have been ousted or are still standing. The most dangerous are the terrorists: for how can you fight someone who is willing, even eagerly *wishing* to die? You have lost the battle in advance. Throw in the promise of fifty virgins delivered to you in so-called Heaven (a heaven that looks much like a brothel, consequently) and the indoctrinated person becomes unbeatable (I keep wondering how one handles fifty virgins: wouldn't at least two or three 'professionals' alleviate the task?).

Such terrorists along with the dictators and religious fanatics are the most famous Arab 'Supermen': Osama Bin Laden, Saddam Hussein, Muammar Gaddafi, Hosni Mubarak, Abdullah bin Abdul Aziz Al Saud, Ayman Al Zawahiri, Mahmoud Ahmadinejad … Of course, some of them are fortunately gone and by the time you read this, more will be. But since they grow and proliferate like yeast, the extinction of the species cannot be counted on.

And let's not overlook the lesser known representatives of the kind. Let's not forget the number one 'Arab Superman' prototypes: the father, the brother, the boyfriend, the husband, the son, the neighbour, the CEO, the priest, the sheikh, the media worker, the advertising copy writer, the politician, the office colleague, etc. In short: the guy next door.

Indeed, Superman is an Arab. He may appear powerful, but his muscles are just a facade for his insecurities. He may seem authentic, but he is actually fake. A pale replica of an original he can't level up to. He may look resistant, but he doesn't last long. A simple challenge can shake him, scare him and break him. Kryptonite is just a green allegory for his countless hidden fears. He may give the impression of being helpful, but he is only smothering and oppressive. He may sound intelligent, but listen to him carefully and you'll see he confuses manhood with machismo, faith with fanaticism, ethics with stale traditions, goodness with self-interest, protection with asphyxiation, love with possession and strength with despotism. He may look nice on the surface, but he is rotten on the inside. Open the shiny shell and you'll find nothing but lies, falseness, cowardice and hypocrisy. He may claim to be saving the world, but the world actually needs to be saved *from* him; and first and foremost, he needs to be saved from himself

But when did this 'Superman pattern' start, really?

All stories have a beginning. A long-lasting, seemingly never-ending story like this one has to have a catchy beginning. Well, it all started like this: first confusion invented fear. Then fear invented God. Then God invented the concept of sin. Then the concept of sin invented the macho man. Then the macho man invented the docile woman. Then the docile woman invented sneakiness. Then sneakiness invented the defensive masks. Then the defensive masks invented the battle of the sexes, and lots of other things in between. Then it all came back to confusion.

Superman is not the only one to blame for his own existence and endurance. Let's not overlook that it is women who breed Supermen originally: the ignorance of mothers, the superficiality of girlfriends, the compliance of daughters, the self-victimisation of sisters, the passivity of wives, and so on and so forth. The admiration of Lois Lane for the bogus, flashy character at the expense of the real, humble one is but a clear and significant example of the role women play in the continuation of the macho race. You see, it's a vicious circle. And many are trapped in it. Men *and* women. Happily so. Unknowingly or deliberately. That is why we need promptly to realise that Superman is a counterfeit man and of the poorest quality. Time for him to rip off the costume and stick to his street clothes. Time for us to scorn glitzy labels and go for the real thing. In ourselves, before anything, and anywhere, and anyone else.

I

Why this book?

> If you do not tell the truth about yourself,
> you cannot tell it about other people.
> *Virginia Woolf*

The poem
Lost and found

The best book I will ever write
is hidden somewhere
under the books I have already written:
I know it.

And maybe
just maybe
if I search well and long enough
I will find it
someday.

… Yet something keeps telling me
that the best book I will ever write
is none other than those black scraps of dirt
stuck under my fingernails:
my stubborn fingernails
never tired of digging.

The rant
In praise of egoism

> That is part of the beauty of all literature. You discover that your
> longings are universal longings, that you're not lonely
> and isolated from anyone. You belong.
>
> *F. Scott Fitzgerald*

Allow me to say it as frankly and bluntly as possible: I don't write because I want to change the world. It is not my key aim to change the world (assuming I could). It is not my key aim, either, to turn the hopeful monotheists into aware atheists. Let the monotheists bathe in the bliss of their illusions. It is not my key aim to convince the machos of the necessity of respecting women and their dignity. The machos' second punishment is that they are machos. As for their first punishment, it is that I, and other women (and men) like me, exist. And we are bound to run into each other at a cross road or two.

It is not my key aim to transform the hypocrites into sincere human beings. The hypocrites are better off rotting in the mud of their lies: those they tell others, but most of all, those they tell themselves. It is not my key aim to expose the dishonesty of most religious representatives. Charlatanism and idiocy deserve each other. It is not my key aim to deconstruct the decayed institution of marriage. May the fervent fans of the 'till death do us part' myth prosper and breed on the bed of their chimeras.

It is not my key aim to persuade the oppressive men that women (body and mind) are not their possession; not as long as some women are persuaded of that as much as men are. It is not my key aim to prove to the burqa ladies that they are subjected to, and brainwashed by, tools of patriarchal oppression. It is not my key aim to prove to the *Playboy* ladies that they are subjected to, and brainwashed by, tools of patriarchal oppression. It is not my key aim to reveal the double standards of our duplicitous societies and systems. The primary condition of the statement 'all human beings are born free and equal in rights' is that we must *first* be human beings. And some people are just not born with that merit.

I swear (not by 'God', no), that it is not my key aim to guide the lost, or to enlighten the blind, or to corrupt the pious, or to soothe the neurotic, or to cure the impotent/frigid. My key aim is *my* right to be whoever I want to be; *my* right to say whatever I want to say; *my* right to take whatever I want to take; and *my* right to do whatever I want to do; notwithstanding the responsibilities that come with those rights, and that I joyfully embrace.

Don't overlook the 'my' above. Notice it well. It is not there by coincidence. Egocentric? So be it. Loud and clear. This is exactly what the world needs in my modest opinion: more earnest egoists and less false altruists and do-gooders.

Yet *if* – while I am being whoever I want to be, and saying whatever I want to say, and taking whatever I want to take, and doing whatever I want to do – I am provoking a few others to also be whoever they want to be, to also say whatever they want to say, to also take whatever they want to take, to also do whatever they want to do … Then I shall consider myself the luckiest person on the face of the Earth. I take so much pride in these 'collateral damages' I cause, and they provide me with strength, determination, tenacity and passion.

Believe me, it is not my key aim to change the world. What I care about is living and writing. That is my main battle. My main cause. My main struggle. Living and writing myself without compromises, without bribes, without deals under the table. Living and writing myself naked: as naked as a poem that has just sprung out of a womb.

And that's about it.

The narrative
Note to the reader

> I have nothing to offer anybody
> except my own confusion.
> *Jack Kerouac*

Dear Reader,

Before you start cumulating all sorts of assumptions and jumping to conclusions, kindly note that, in spite of the flaming title, this is not a manifesto against men in general. Nor is it a manifesto against Arab men in particular.

It is, however, a howl in the face of the patriarchal system and its absurd, not to mention shameful 'values', commodities and references: a howl written with passion, *not* venom. It is also a howl in the face of one particular infamous by-product of that system: the macho species, the narrow-minded species, the Neanderthal species, the 'you only exist in my shadow' species …

We'd like to think this species is extinct, but it is not. We'd like to think the Arab revolutions are about to bring an end to it, but nothing is more uncertain, as one monster seems to be replacing another. We'd like to think it is disappearing, but it is not even endangered.

It is everywhere, still. Prowling like a silent ogre. Despite all the fights for women's rights, despite the demonstrations, the laws, the civil liberties granted, the so-called 'wind of change', the seeming equality in some parts of the planet. I like to compare it to Dante's hell: some are trapped in the first circle, others in the ninth. But it is still an *inferno*.

You might argue that there are many women out there who are a fetid product of the patriarchal system as well. And you'd be absolutely right: I couldn't agree more, and I insist on repeating that fact every time I can, in order to overcome the easy, treacherous and widespread confusion between 'patriarchal' and 'male'. I am talking here about women who feel that the more a guy ignores them or mistreats them, the more attractive he becomes; women who choose alpha males over decent, respectful men; women who wish for baby boys instead of baby girls once they are pregnant; women who educate their sons to be macho and their daughters to be tameable and tame; women who keep silent when these daughters are abused, whether physically or psychologically; women who drag these daughters to hymen reconstruction surgeries or genital mutilation procedures; women who preach to other women about how they were made to stay home and *not* participate in the political or social or business lives of their countries; women who teach other women obedience and submission; women who disdain or hate or fight successful women; women who do not *believe* in successful women; women who encourage their girls to get married at fourteen or to be 'patient' when their husbands beat them; but first and foremost: women who are truly and deeply convinced that men are the stronger, superior, brighter sex … The ugly manifestations of the patriarchal female (whether conscious or unconscious) in our societies and cultures are infinite.

On the other hand, and in every corner of this modern world, there are still men who think they are 'better' than women and state it by pounding their own chests like gorillas: men who mistreat women. Men who beat up women. Men who exploit women. Men who patronise women. Men who underestimate women. Men who cover up women. Men who treat women like cheap pieces of meat. Men who 'sell' and 'buy' women. Men who look down on women and are condescending with them at best. Men who use their muscles and/or the power (social, political, religious, economic) guaranteed to them by a corrupt patriarchal system to oppress women. Supermen, as they like to see themselves. 'Saviours' of humanity.

But Superman, again, is a lie. And the only thing that needs to be saved today is the sinking ship called manhood. Yes. Superman is a lie: a distasteful, dangerous, poisoning, if not suicidal one. As distasteful, dangerous and poisoning as the 'damsel in distress' cliché. And as much as the 'persecuted' or 'self-hating' maiden needs to start believing in her own powers, the pseudo *Übermensch* also needs to start becoming a man. A real one:

The man that femininity deserves. The man that humanity deserves. But first and foremost, the man that he himself deserves to be.

2

How it all started (in general)

Then if I am an experiment, am I the whole of it? No,
I think not; I think the rest of it is part of it.
I am the main part of it, but I think the rest
of it has its share in the matter.

Mark Twain (Eve's Diary)

The poem
Beginning again

Then God created the woman in his image,
created her from raw earth,
created her from the idea of herself:
Lilith,
in whose eyes you see love lost
or love abandoned.

Lilith, the huntress and the hunted,
who coos like a dove to tame the lion,
who makes laws and breaks them,
who binds her men, then weeps for their release,
who stands at the Earth's centre
    and watches it turn slowly round her,
who takes to herself the cypress, the dusk
    and the far reaches of the sea.

Lilith, who is nameless to us,
whose future already shines in her mind's eye,
who is strong in her womanhood and therefore mild,
who eats the sky and drinks the moon like milk,
who is one minute in your arms,
the next a distant shadow.

Lilith, whose nakedness
can only be seen by those who do not look
the liberated woman, the woman in chains,
the woman who is free even from freedom,
the tip where hell and heaven meet in peace,
desire itself and the longing for desire.

Lilith, tender in victory, powerful in defeat,
who speaks for any woman,
who speaks for every man,
who saw but never chose,
who chose but never put to waste.

Lilith, quick to betray her sex,
quick to betray,
whose thousand cuts
are more tender than a thousand kisses.

Lilith, poet-demon, demon-poet,
find her in me, find her in dreams,
find her and take from her
whatever you want,
take all,
take everything,
it will never be enough.

The rant
Heads or tails

> Alas! It is not the child but the boy
> that generally survives in the man.
> *Arthur Helps*

Some men tell a woman: 'I respect you, support you, am in solidarity with you and will protect you for as long as you live. This is God's command, and it is your right to expect this from us.' But they confuse respect with condescension, support with repression and solidarity with an insulting pat on the shoulder. They confuse, especially, the commands of their patriarchal god with the crushing of some of the most basic human rights.

Some men who claim they 'respect, support, are in solidarity with, and protect the woman', tell her: 'We encourage our partners to have successful careers. Your ambitions are our ambitions and your achievements are a source of pride to us.' But deep down they are convinced that a woman only works to fill her spare time. They suffer a heart attack if she brings in more money than they do; and she often has to beg confidence and approval from them, as if she were a little child imploring their attention.

Some men who claim they 'encourage their partners to have successful careers' tell a woman: 'We are aroused by sharp intelligence, strong personalities and fiery tempers. What's the point in a woman being beautiful if she's a cold little doll that doesn't react to our words? We even admire the way you argue with us and scold us.' But they wish in secret that women were less intelligent and impetuous, and more obedient and passive.

Some men who claim they 'are aroused by sharp intelligence, strong personalities and fiery tempers' tell a woman: 'We love your sexual appetite and your burning libido. You always pre-empt our desires, and light up our beds with new fantasies.' But they can't bear the thought of her not being a virgin on their wedding night, feel offended if she takes the initiative, and consider their honour to be tied up exclusively with what lies between her thighs.

Some men who claim they 'love a woman's sexual appetite and burning libido' tell her: 'We can't abide jealousy and accept no justification for it. We are not each other's possessions and we must naturally trust each other.' But while they see nothing wrong with fucking or marrying another, they would not hesitate to trash, leave, beat, or in some cases even murder her, if she cheats on them, because what applies to them obviously does not apply to her.

Some men who claim they 'can't abide jealousy and accept no justification for it' tell a woman: 'We can't get enough of listening to you. Please always share with us your fears, your feelings, your problems, and your worries.' But whenever she opens her mouth, they actually think: 'When will this boring flood of confessions end?'

Some men who claim they 'can't get enough of listening to a woman' tell her: 'We place your pleasure at the top of our priorities; we are not selfish and we don't care for one-sided sex.' But they often fall into deep sleep on the way back from their sexual journey, even before she has set off on hers.

Some men who claim they 'place a woman's pleasure at the top of their priorities' tell her: 'We value your vulnerability. With us, you don't have to pretend to be always strong and self-confident. Don't be afraid of taking your mask off and revealing your fragile face. We love you whether you are triumphant and victorious, or defeated and weeping.' But they do not hesitate to fight her, when necessary, with their detailed knowledge of her insecurities and weak spots.

Some men who claim they 'value a woman's vulnerability' tell her: 'We love you just the way you are. Don't change a thing. We adore every detail of your natural beauty, free of any interference.' But when that natural woman sneaks into their dreams, she sees ghosts of other women: women who don't look like her. Women who are happy to be dolls and accessories. Women who don't mind always saying 'yes'. Women who never argue or challenge. Women with artificial bodies and empty gazes. Women who sail confidently in the waters of the masculine subconscious. Women-things who wander content, fearless, immune, eternal … and lifeless.

The narrative

Genesis, not the way they'd like to think it occurred

> The end is where we start from.
> *T. S. Eliot*

… And there was evening, and there was morning – the sixth day. Then God said: 'Let there be Man, and let him rule over the fish of the sea and the birds of the air, over all the Earth and over all the creatures that move along the ground.' And there was Man. And God named him Adam. Then God saw what he had made, and he thought it was all very good …

Except for one problem. Man was immortal. And unhappy about it. For it hadn't occurred to God, who was everlasting, to say the least, that Man needed closure. But Man did. So God leaned on a huge rock (the same one he had created on the first day) and started reflecting upon the problem. 'Aren't the animals enough? Aren't the plants and the mountains and the rivers enough? What more should I do to keep this irritating creature off my back?'

Then God, just like Archimedes, had a Eureka moment. He shall give Man Death. And God created cigarettes, car accidents, earthquakes and other relieving nuisances. Then God saw what he had made, and obviously, he thought it was all very good …

Except for a second problem. Man was insufferably arrogant. For it hadn't occurred to God, who was the One and Only, and keen on staying so, to say the least, that Man needed to realise his limits. But Man did. So God dived in a deep blue sea (the same one he had created on the second day) and went on reflecting upon the problem. 'Aren't the animals and the plants and the mountains and the rivers and death enough? What more should I do to keep this annoying creature off my back?'

Then God had a second Eureka moment. He shall give Man

self-consciousness. And God created mirrors. Then God saw what he had made, and obviously, he thought it was all very good …

Except for a third problem. Man was severely depressed. For it hadn't occurred to God, who was as cheerful and optimistic as Bugs Bunny, to say the least, that Man needed solace. But Man did. So God strolled the moon (the same one he had created on the third day) and went on reflecting upon the problem. 'Aren't the animals and the plants and the mountains and the rivers and death and mirrors enough? What more should I do to keep this grumpy creature off my back?'

Then God had a third Eureka moment. He shall give Man chemical consolation. And God created Prozac. Then God saw what he had made, and obviously, he thought it was all very good …

Except for a fourth problem. Man was bored. For it hadn't occurred to God, who was self-satisfied and auto-sufficient, to say the least, that Man needed entertainment. But Man did. So God rode a zebra (the same one he had created on the fourth day) and went on reflecting upon the problem. 'Aren't the animals and the plants and the mountains and the rivers and death and mirrors and Prozac enough? What more should I do to keep this whining creature off my back?'

Then God had a fourth Eureka moment. He shall give Man something to play with. So God took another piece of clay from the ground (not big enough, unfortunately), moulded it into a tube, and stuck it over the man's crotch – where it would come in quite 'handy', he cleverly foresaw. And God created Man's penis. Then God saw what he had made, and obviously, he thought it was very good …

Except for a fifth problem. Man was lonely. For it hadn't occurred to God, who was an adept of solitary pleasures, to say the least, that Man needed companionship. But Man did. And Man was making it quite clear to God's ill-tempered ears: sighing at night, grumbling by day, complaining 24/7. It was intolerable.

So God sat down under a fig tree (the same one he had created on the fifth day) and went on reflecting upon the problem. 'Aren't the animals and the plants and the mountains and the rivers and death and mirrors and Prozac and the penis enough? What more should I do to keep this exasperating creature off my back?'

Then God had a fifth Eureka moment. He shall give Man, and his penis, someone to play with. Someone to give orders to. Someone to look down on. Someone to be served by. Someone to use and abuse. Hence God, instead of resting on the seventh day, like it was meant to be, made one last effort, and created Woman. He created her from earth, just like he did with Man. And he named her Lilith. Then God saw what he had made, and obviously, obviously – given the curves and the rest – he thought it was remarkably good …

Except for one last big problem. Lilith did not come out a toy, as it was initially intended. Or, at least, she was the failed project of a toy. For she came as an independent, strong female, who took no bullshit from Man (nor from God, for that matter). She was a 'partner', and did not like being treated as an accessory. So after having had enough of the silly, gratuitous do this's and do thats, she decided to leave so-called paradise for a more interesting place. She came down to Earth. And started breeding.

But then Man went back to whining and complaining from solitude. So God made a second attempt at Woman. Except that this time, in order to make sure she'd be obedient and submissive, he had the genius idea of creating her from Man's rib: a tiny part of the masculine whole. How could she not be, therefore, docile and compliant to her 'master'? And that's how Eve was created.

… And from that moment on, it was the end of Man and Woman, and the beginning of an absurd mayhem called 'gender conflict'.

3

How it all started (for me)

In love the paradox occurs that two beings
become one and yet remain two.

Erich Fromm

The poem
A love metaphor

Love is a slippery fish.
Only it smells better.

Love is a slippery fish.
Every time you think you caught it,
it slides away.
And when it finally rests tranquil in your hand,
don't sigh with relief:
it only means
it is dead.

The rant
In and out

> It is not the men in my life.
> It is the life in my men.
> *Mae West*

I once fell in love with a guy because he treated me like a queen
Then I fell out of love because he was not a king.

I once fell in love with a guy because he made me laugh
Then I fell out of love because he didn't drink my tears when I cried.

I once fell in love with a guy because he was a good speaker
Then I fell out of love because he talked much but said little.

I once fell in love with a guy because he took me to the moon
Then I fell out of love because he didn't know how to bring me
back to Earth.

I once fell in love with a guy because I enjoyed sleeping with him
Then I fell out of love because I did not enjoy sleeping next to him.

I once fell in love with a guy because I had a crush on him
Then I fell out of love because he had a crush on himself.

I once fell in love with a guy because he did something right
Then I fell out of love because he did everything else wrong.

I once fell in love with a guy because he knew how to touch my
body
Then I fell out of love because he did not know how to touch
my soul.

I once fell in love with a guy because he knew how to touch my
soul
Then I fell out of love because he did not know how to touch
my body.

I once fell in love with a guy because I felt comfortable with him
Then I fell out of love because I felt too comfortable with him.

I once fell in love with a guy because he was smart and
cultivated
Then I fell out of love because he bragged about being smart
and cultivated.

I once fell in love with a guy because he made me dream about
him
Then I fell out of love because I got sick of dreaming.

I once fell in love with a guy because he knew how to walk into
my life
Then I fell out of love because he did not know when to leave.

I once fell in love with a guy because he was cute and sexy
Then I fell out of love because he, too, thought he was cute and
sexy.

I once fell in love with a guy because he wrote me nice letters
Then I fell out of love because his words did not become flesh.

I once fell in love with a guy because he looked up to me
Then I fell out of love because I did not look up to him.

I once fell in love with a guy because he was perfect
Then I fell out of love because he was perfect.

In and out
fire after fire,
in and out
ashes to ashes,
and the one to keep me burning
is yet to be invented.
The one to keep me burning
is yet to be found.

The narrative

Close encounters with the second kind

> All women become like their mothers. That is their tragedy.
> No man does. That's his.
>
> *Oscar Wilde*

He looked a lot like Tintin, the famous French comic book character. He had delicate features, a cute snobbish nose, and a malicious smile. We were both seven when he joined my all-girls Catholic school. He was one of three boys living in the neighbourhood whose parents managed to convince the nuns to accept them as students, given that 'a boy that age cannot seriously represent a menace to a little girl's virtue'. Says who?

I liked Jacques right away. And I knew he liked me too because, even though he hardly ever spoke to me, he seized every opportunity to pull my long hair and run away. It hurt a lot at times, to the point of tears, which made me like Jacques even more. The harder he pulled, the more I liked him, and the more I was sure he liked me. It was a very innate and instinctive certainty, because obviously, I did not have at that time any knowledge of relationship politics. I couldn't possibly have translated his behaviour into a logic that stated: 'He is pulling my hair because he is frustrated. He is frustrated because he likes me, thus it makes him feel scared.' Much later, I understood that this was a typical male pattern – if there are any – with different ways to 'pull a woman's hair'.

'I want to marry that guy!' I used to tell my mother whenever we stood on the balcony and I saw our tall, handsome young neighbour crossing the street, some 15 metres down. I did not know his name, but I wanted to marry him. I was no more than nine years old, but I wanted to marry him. It was a mystery to Mom: one of her daughter's many weird stances and actions, to which she was only beginning to become accustomed. Then she had the terrible idea of stopping that same young man on the street one day, while I was with her, and telling him about my caprice. 'Oh that's so cute,' he said, pinching my crimson, mortified I-wish-I-could-die-right-now cheek. I hated him at once. And I stopped telling my mother I wanted to marry him. She was puzzled. But one day, after she had asked me why for the hundredth time, I told her: 'Because he is not far away any more.' Obviously, she couldn't understand. Nor could I, but that's how I felt. I wanted 'the distant man'. I needed the 'out of reach'; the dream, basically.

The above happened almost at the same time that I started having my recurrent childhood nightmare. I was in my small white wooden bed. Suddenly the bed was thrown from the fifth floor, and I could see it, and me lying down on it, dropping vertically, yet slowly, to the bottom. Then the bed would ascend the five floors again and take its place in the room. But not for long. It was tossed down again and again by some mysterious force. As if I were Sisyphus *and* the rock, simultaneously.

Was that nightmare an allegory for my restless soul? A soul standing on the edge, forever on the edge? One that doesn't settle, that is addicted to beginnings, that never stops commencing almost everything all over again, that incessantly yearns for the 'out of reach'? Was I an example of what French poet André Breton said: 'All my life, my heart has yearned for a thing I cannot name'? It might very well be so, but it was tremendously disturbing for the little girl I was back then.

What is certain, though, is that the nightmare could definitely be seen as a premature parable for my relationship with men: build, destroy, rebuild. Build, destroy, rebuild. Over and over again, until one of us is completely worn out, until one of us sur-renders to the impossibility of going on. The circle of life? Rather a life in circles. A heart in circles. A will in circles. No dead end. But no end either. No mediocre reality. But, also, no reality.

It all culminated when I hit twelve and had my shocking encounter with De Sade's writings, added to my parents' deteriorating marriage and daily fighting. That is when I started firmly believing, against all odds and dreamy girlfriends, that there is no Mr Right, just a Mr Right Now. No knight in shining armour, no Prince Charming, no 'happily ever after'.

Carpe diem. Everything comes with an expiry date. Especially relationships. It would have been hard to find a more cynical and disenchanted teenager. My favourite reads at bedtime? *Philosophy in the Bedroom* and *Venus in Furs*.

Most of my adult life has been, because of that, a useless walk in loops. In fact, I have been a head-on warrior on many levels, except in matters of the heart. I have been the queen of plan Bs in love.

I never got to the end of plan A. I automatically assumed plan A wouldn't work and I moved onto plan B. As for plan B, it didn't matter if it didn't work either. For there was always a plan C. Yes. I have been the queen of plan Bs, Cs, Ds, etc.

My friends used to call me wise. Visionary. Alert. Farsighted. Sceptical. Or plain bitch for turning my back on men without a second glance. But why do I have a hunch that I have just been a coward? A woman holding a hand bomb which is none other than herself, hoping it/she will not explode in her own face one day. Or else, what do you call someone who uses the fire exit even when there is no fire?

Obviously, it didn't help at all that I got married at twenty to someone I had met when I was only sixteen. Marriage was then my only ticket out of my parents' house and a first step towards me becoming 'my own boss'. It did not help, either, that I was a virgin bride (shame, shame) and that he and I did not click sexually. A person should not walk into a marriage without having experienced intimacy with the 'chosen one' (as a matter of fact, a person should preferably not walk into a marriage at all, but I'll deal with that later). It might seem to many of you as if I am stating something self-evident (the necessity of experiencing pre-marital sex), but it was not like that in Lebanon in the late eighties. Hell, it is not even like that in Lebanon now. In recent video reportage conducted in Beirut by London-based Lebanese producer Amanda Homsi-Ottosson (Black Unicorn Productions), most of the twenty-something guys asked if they'd marry a woman who was not a virgin answered that they wouldn't. And the survey was done with college students. In 2011. In a country described as the 'Switzerland of the Middle East'.

Soon after the unlucky first experience, both my husband and I turned into chronic unsatisfied adulterers, always looking for more, for the 'greener grass on the other side'. As you might imagine, I resent the word 'adulterer' because of its religious connotation (I prefer the expression 'serial lover'), but I don't mind using it, especially since it makes so many Arab eyes roll with social prejudice: you know, we are famous for stoning (whether literally or metaphorically) that species in its female manifestation and celebrating it in its male version (the Whore vs. Casanova syndrome). It doesn't matter if most people are doing *it* in secret and decrying *it* in public; it doesn't matter if this double life represents for a large number of couples a 'practical' solution instead of going through a thorny religious divorce process or jeopardising their social status. But it's fine. I've always believed that being ostracised in a phoney two-faced society is the best thing that could happen to me. And I have to admit I have done a lot to make it happen: I have struggled to be able to live loyal to myself and to my views, and not as others would like to see me.

My sense of self was never wrapped up in what family, friends, men, society, etc. thought of me. And I have fiercely avoided weighing/measuring my worth in the eyes of others, because that is the real act of 'adultery' – being a traitor to oneself. And like my dear Marquis wrote: 'My manner of thinking, so you say, cannot be approved? Do you suppose I care? A poor fool indeed is he who adopts a manner of thinking for others.'

Clearly, at a certain point I'd had enough of the 'double life' and decided it was time to be even truer to myself, and face divorce as a risk of every marriage. It simply comes with the territory (apart from some happy exceptions that only serve to prove the rule). Never mind if people in my country still treat divorced women condescendingly, either with disrespect and bigotry or with pity (it is almost always *her* fault if the marriage fails). I'd also had enough of indulging men by faking orgasms in order to reassure them: I am in 'this' for *me*, as much as, if not more than, I am in it for them. And the only way for them to feel reassured is to really please me. It has to be a very well earned (mutual) reward.

In my blind quest, I have been with many men. Tall men. Short men. Fat men. Fit men. Young men. Old men. Funny men. Serious men. Nice men. Naughty men. Hard-working men. Lazy men. Creative men. Rational men. Loquacious men. Silent men. Elegant men. Hippie men. Smiling men. Frowning men. Quick men. Slow men. Depraved men. Deprived men. Warrior men. Diplomatic men. Furious men. Serene men. Ambitious men. Desperate men …

But every time, I was able to look ahead and see exactly how each guy was going to disappoint me ('a self-defence mechanism due to your fear of attachment/intimacy/commitment', psychologists would comment); and every time, I ended up discovering that those men were indeed 'enemies'. Not *my* enemies. No. But enemies of *themselves*. And that is why walking away was so easy.

But how could most men not be their own enemies, really? There are so many (ridiculous or terrorising) expectations of them since early childhood; not to mention the awful gender conditioning that comes with the expectations (blue/pink, strong/weak, active/passive, hunter/prey, achiever/receiver, etc). There is so much pressure applied on them to live up to an impossible fantasy: 'Boys are tough. Boys don't cry. Boys don't lose a fight. Boys fear nothing. Boys go to war. Boys must have a spectacular hard on when "show time" arrives. Boys do not get attached. Boys always have to prove that they are "manly".' And what is the first characteristic of being manly? *Not* being sensitive, of course.

But boys are indeed scared. And sensitive. That's the reality. And they have the *right* to be scared and need to embrace their sensitivity and reject this counter-productive Superman ideal. It is only then that a real change can start to happen in relationship dynamics, breaking the deteriorating moulds and prototypes.

Girls need to begin conceiving of themselves as competent and influential instead of mere victims; boys need to begin conceiving of themselves as human and humane beings: vulnerable, genuine anti-heroes, and not invincible champions.

Unfortunately, we all know how sensitive guys in this world treat a woman decently only to get dumped for a macho hard dick that treats her like shit. I am talking about educated, liberated women, who have sensitive, nice guys for friends, lovers and husbands at home … There is something deeply wrong in the female human psyche that keeps alpha male arseholes supplied with a constant line of available and willing women. Lois Lane is an example of a very common female phenomenon. And this is the reason why women have to do their part in the process of change as well. It all makes me think about how us women are taught/trained, consciously or unconsciously (no big difference), to admire/love/pursue our tormentors (that's where the famous Stockholm Syndrome started). It makes me think about how I, for example, used to have an embarrassing sexual attraction towards ego-driven predatory males, the same men that I loathed when I used my brain instead of my libido: there was an aspect of the male arrogance that I was attracted to (and I am not ashamed to admit that I still love a tiny bit of that arrogance on occasion, as long as it does not cross the limit of my own ego and dignity). It also makes me think about masochistic tendencies and how they can ruin a relationship (and a whole life) if they become part of an emotionally destructive pattern, instead of part of a mere sexual game between two consenting adults.

On this last subject, I can't easily explain why I have such an intense passion for the Marquis de Sade, beyond how much it means to me that he liberated me as a writer and the fact that he never distinguished between normal and abnormal behaviour in sexuality: a major part of my philosophy of life and writing. Still, my love for him is seen by many as an aberration, since he is considered *the* misogynist writer par excellence. But I chose not to see him as a misogynist. To me, he cannot be reduced to an obsessive hater of women who enjoyed torturing them on paper. He was a bold adventurer of the human soul, one who dug in it deeper than anybody else, even to this day. Plus, I believe that erotic imagination does not (and should not) submit to gender politics. The principle of equality between men and women when transposed to the arena of sex can sometimes be a burden or an inhibitor, and is not necessarily a way to sexual excitement. That is why many powerful and achieved women have sexual fantasies involving submission and S&M, and like to play at surrendering. It's the erotic wish to be beyond will and beyond thought. The expressions 'politically incorrect' or 'discriminative' or 'not allowed' do not have any place between two consenting adults in bed, as long as there is no extrapolation, and both man and woman are aware that 'what happens in bed, stays in bed'.

It certainly did not improve the situation that I was turned off, body and mind, by all the disgusting double standards that I was witnessing almost everywhere around me, while meeting self-proclaimed superheroes and/or cowards in denial. But I was okay with it. With *them*, I mean. No big expectations = no disappointments. It's a safe formula, right?

However, as soon as I hit my forties (wouldn't it be more accurate to say: as soon as my forties hit me?), I thought: 'I've been fasting for forty years. Where the hell is that tempting devil?' As soon as I hit my forties, I got sick of the safe formulas, sick of the Mr Right Nows, and I started yearning for a 'unsafe' leap; I started yearning for a Mr Right. And that's when I decided to stop being disenchanted beforehand in relationships. I decided that between 'careless' and 'carefree' is an abyss I would have to cross, bleeding yet unharmed. I decided that I'd much rather regret the things I did than the things I did not do. I also decided: 'No more hit and runs. Now I want to hit and stand trial. Guilty as charged, eyes wide open.'

It wouldn't take many men to prove me wrong: just one. It would take a lot to prove me wrong: *the* one. The one who could unintentionally sabotage my intentional sabotaging.

But aren't we supposed to lose our illusions with age? Am I growing up backwards? Either that or fairy tales are an inevitable human weakness. A bit like being schizophrenic if you're Lebanese: it sort of comes with the package.

Despite all the early cynicism, this is how I have come to think of it: we are only halves. At best. Sometimes just bits and pieces. Yet the question is not: 'Where is the other half?'

It rather is: 'Is there another half?' Do we believe in it and try to figure it out or do we just look away? Safe or sorry? There must be a third alternative out there. There *must* be.

Don't get me wrong: I have not grown into a soggy romantic. I still want to find my 'Marquis de Sade'. But now I want to fall in love with him. And knowing myself, I should add: for a bit longer than two weeks.

4

The disastrous invention of monotheism

The real axis of evil is Christianity, Judaism, and Islam.
Organised religion is the main source of hatred in the world:
It is violent, irrational, intolerant, allied to racism, tribalism, and
bigotry, invested in ignorance and hostile to free inquiry,
contemptuous of women and coercive toward children.
Christopher Hitchens

The poem
Saying grace

Thank you God
for the tsunami in Indonesia,
for Hurricane Katrina,
and for the last earthquake in Japan.

Thank you for World War I,
for World War II,
and for whatever sequels you'll be sending us
next Christmas.

Thank you God
for the babies dying from hunger in Africa,
for the babies dying from hatred in Palestine.

Thank you for George W. Bush, Mahmoud Ahmadinejad
and for that sweet Adolf Hitler.

Thank you for volcanic eruptions, cyclones and meteorite
impacts;
for Hiroshima, Chernobyl and the Qana massacre;
for Aids, cancer and Parkinson's.

Thank you God
for blindness, for car accidents,
for racists, rapists and paedophiles.

And thank you for nuns
and thank you for priests
and thank you for ayatollahs
and thank you for Wahhabists.

Thank you for cholera and plane crashes,
for orphans, widows and child beggars.
Thank you for land mines
and for all the amazing toys
of mass destruction.

Oh and before I forget:
Thank you thank you for the ozone hole
(I've been craving a darker tan).

Then thank you God for Al Qaeda,
for the burqa and for *Playboy*,
Thank you for women's oppression, for honour crimes,
for vengeance, and for injustice.

Thank you for heartbreaks, betrayals and disappointments,

for fake promises and stolen dreams.
Thank you for nightmares
and for the real lives that look like these.

Thank you for narrow-minded people,
and the stupid and the cruel.
Thank you for backstabbers, for wife beaters,
for Wall Street sharks and serial killers.

Thank you for cockroaches and dictators:
(So good to know they'd survive a nuclear bomb).

Thank you God
for Judgement day, for fast food,
for body hair and small penises.
And thank you for marriage, and thank you for hell:
(These two are such a nice touch).

But most of all, dear God,
Thank you for God.
For of all the disasters you drew,
your real masterpiece
is YOU.

The rant
Why not

> I cannot believe in a God who wants
> to be praised all the time.
> *Friedrich Nietzsche*

I don't believe in God because I'd rather be handcuffed by my lover than by an illusion.

I don't believe in God because I prefer to trip over and limp while walking, instead of using overrated crutches.

I don't believe in God because I like to make up my own rules (and then break them).

I don't believe in God because I don't want a Big Brother to watch over me.

I don't believe in God because I wish to be good for goodness' sake, not because of some post-death rewarding process.

I don't believe in God because I wish to be deterred from evil by my basic human decency, not by the threat of being fried.

I don't believe in God because I am not an adept of monologues and one-way conversations.

I don't believe in God because I favour life-improving inventions.

I don't believe in God because I don't want to postpone Hell and Paradise. I'd much rather live them here and now.

I don't believe in God because if he really did exist and everything in this world happens according to his will, then he doesn't deserve my faith in him after all.

I don't believe in God because I am a woman, and he opted to see me as a rib not as a whole.

I don't believe in God because I learnt to pat my own back and to wag my own finger in my face.

I don't believe in God because he did a pretty lousy job of choosing his representatives for someone who is 'omnipotent'.

I don't believe in God because I know perfectly well how to mess myself up all by myself.

I don't believe in God because I support freedom and choice over intimidation and bribe.

I don't believe in God because every suffering child on this planet makes it harder for me to believe in him.

I don't believe in God because he needs to be feared and adored, which proves an immense lack of self-confidence.

I don't believe in God because I am my own god.
And I'd rather believe in myself.

The narrative

Thou shalt not covet thy neighbour's wife nor donkey

All right, then, I'll go to hell.

Mark Twain

Between a mother who dragged me to mass every Sunday morning and a squad of nuns who dragged us students to mass every Wednesday afternoon, I was trapped in a suffocating state of 'holy bliss'. I knew the Catholic liturgy and rites by heart (I still do). But that was far from being enough to make a fervent devotee out of wicked me.

I used the school's mass period to revise my studies or to read my favourite books. Whenever that was possible, I used to choose a quiet corner in church, supposedly to favour my spiritual contemplation and my (much needed) act of penitence. Then I'd hide a good novel inside the big prayer book that we were all given to follow the ceremony and I'd mumble the sacred words with my lips, like a robot, all while reading intently (multitasking is indeed a feminine art). By the age of thirteen, my utmost pleasure was to read strictly debauched literature during mass (transgression is, on the other hand, a Catholic art). In fact, every time I found a 'bad' book in my dad's library, I'd keep it aside for church reading. Talk about sweet revenge.

I also used to have lots of fun fabricating sins for the confessional ritual. It was one excellent way to work out my imagination. Yet it mustn't have been a treat for the poor priest to listen to my weekly delirium and phantasms. One day, as I had just finished the novel *Emmanuelle: The Joys of a Woman* by Emmanuelle Arsan, I went and told him I had kissed one of my classmates on her lips (a pure invention, I'm sad to clarify). I could feel his breath getting faster and heavier as I was recounting the fictitious details of how the Devil had tempted the chaste fourteen-year-old girl that I was.

On another occasion, I confessed to him that I'd been having 'evil' questions on my mind. Asked what they were, I replied: 'Do nuns masturbate? And if they do, is that considered a sin and a breach of the "vow of chastity"?' Despite the screen that was separating us, I saw him almost jump on his chair. I can't remember what he told me or how many Hail Marys I had to recite in order to get the coveted redemption, but I could hardly keep myself from laughing out loud.

Bless me Father for I haven't sinned enough … yet.

That being 'confessed', allow me at this point to refresh your memories with the following:

1 'For the man is not of the woman: but the woman of the man. Neither was the man created for the woman; but the woman for the man.' The New Testament (1 Corinthians 11:8–9)

2 'Blessed are You, King of the universe, for not having made me a woman.' The Siddur (Jewish prayer book)

3 'Men are the protectors and maintainers of women, because Allah has given the one more strength than the other, and because they support them from their means. Therefore the righteous women are devoutly obedient, and guard in the husband's absence what Allah would have them guard. As to those women on whose part ye fear disloyalty and ill conduct, admonish them first, next refuse to share their beds, and last beat them.' The Qur'an (The Women: 34)

The above are excerpts from well-known books, which I assume most of us are familiar with. These are books promoting the three monotheist religions, and competing, as we have just seen, on enforcing patriarchal standards – humiliating women, classifying them as men's property and oppressing them.

Some would react: 'These are only excerpts. It is scientifically inaccurate and intellectually dishonest to generalise from details.' A protest to which I'd reply: 'You are right. But even a meticulous reading of these and other books and their teachings will only reveal – in the best case scenario – a certain "indulgence" and tolerance towards women ("they" like to call it respect), an indulgence and tolerance that do not cancel out the arrogance of the above, but in fact emerge from an insulting conviction of superiority that is just as harsh as straight-to-the-point discrimination.'

Others may object: 'These books are all extremely old and reflect different social circumstances in which this kind of discourse was somehow justifiable.' To which I'd respond: 'So be it. Let us suppose I concur, as a good devil's advocate, with the legitimacy of such an objection, and that I can overcome the initial fallacy. But, if this is really the case, then why do these books continue – into our twenty-first century – to be foundational texts that dictate the behaviours, thoughts, principles and the lifestyles of so many people? Why are these texts still untouchable? What internal reform effort has actually led to any change in the woman's image from the perspective of the organised monotheist religions, and contributed to recovering her dignity and equality with men, not just in words, but also – and especially – in deeds?

Too vague? Let me give myself as an example and ask the following question: I am a Lebanese woman, but am I a Lebanese citizen? No, not as long as the religion I was assigned to at birth (neither of us chose the other) is what rules my situation, affairs, position and life, from the cradle to the grave. No, not given I was registered in the official registry as a Catholic, married for the first time in the Catholic Church, and had children whose first description is that they are Catholics. No, not as long as I can't travel abroad with my kids without permission from their father, while he can leave the country with them whenever he wants, without my permission. No, not as long as our great cabinet is almost devoid of women. No, not as long as Lebanese women are denied the right to give their nationality to their children and spouses. No, not as long as the Lebanese political/religious leaders refuse to enact laws targeting men who beat their wives. Not, not as long as the same political/religious leaders refuse to criminalise marital rape, claiming 'such a thing does not exist' (which means that a man has the absolute right to dispose of his wife's body however and whenever he deems fit).

We Lebanese are not 'citizens', not as long as we allow ourselves to this day to ask each other, 'what's your religion?' Not as long as we continue to spread sectarianism, to despise 'the other' (who is this other, I wonder?), and practise chauvinism and discrimination. Not as long as we are an assemblage of confessions, not a nation. Not as long as the political life in this country continues to be run according to its leaders' religious affiliations. Not as long as we have a stone-age law that allows the imprisonment of homosexuals for no other reason than their sexual choice, which is condemned by religion. Not when this oasis of opposition and freedom in the fifties and sixties has become an oasis for oppressors. Not as long as people have to travel to Cyprus in order to marry in a civil ceremony, a marriage that our state recognises (and that our travel agencies promote on billboards) but that is not available here: one of the many manifestations of the great duplicity that we suffer from; and of which I could give countless examples.

Shame on a country that claims to be a 'democratic republic', but lacks a secular civil society freed from the rule of religious figures and laws. And don't tell me about how much Lebanon represents an 'illuminating modern' exception in the region:

somehow people who do that tend to compare it to countries like Saudi Arabia. But isn't a comparison with who/what is 'worse' a form of cowardice and denial? Wouldn't it be more honourable to compare ourselves with the 'better' and thus try to improve, instead of feeling a lame illusory satisfaction?

Also, don't tell me about all the 'delicate balances' that should be taken into consideration in multi-confessional Lebanon. This is nothing but a justification of further feudalism, divisiveness and immorality. This is nothing but allowing religions to monopolise our lives, and legitimising their political, social and economic influence over us.

So, let's get to the core of the matter: can we be Christians, Muslims or Jews, and fight patriarchy and defend gender equality from within our religions? Answering 'yes' is nothing but one of the many expressions of the denial we are living in. These three religions have the same attitude towards women: oppressive and misogynic. How could it not be so, when all three of them were born in the Mediterranean Basin, a geographical and social region where patriarchal values are entrenched? It is very much like two monsters that feed on each other, and that perpetuate themselves through people's ignorance and fears. Like Belgian historian Anne Morelli says: 'The millenary sustainability of religions is only due to their opportune invasion of infantile consciousnesses and their permanent violation of freedom by forced information, which is the characteristic of all conditioning.'

Obviously, monotheist religions did not invent patriarchy: it existed long before they did. But they institutionalised it and strengthened it, instead of trying to end it, and that is a reason good enough for me, as a woman, to fight and reject them. If the God they have invented was really as 'merciful', as 'compassionate', as 'gracious' and as 'just' as they all claim *Him* to be (and don't get me started on the male nature of their deity), wasn't He supposed to have established an equal vision of humankind?

Not only are the organised religions biased against women, but they are, all three of them, racist, sexist, homophobic, merciless, bloody, and biased against humanity, freedom and human rights. They are even biased against common sense. They are ManMade and PowerMade institutions that aim at controlling people and their lives. All of them have, throughout their history, used wars and terrorism to promote their objectives and survive the secular forces that threaten their continued existence, not to mention that their exclusivism has frequently fostered violence against those that are considered outsiders.

Many link this use of violence strictly to Islam, but that's twisting history and reality. Almost everybody in the world has heard of Al Qaeda and Hizbollah, but how many have heard of Hutaree, a Christian militia group involved in many violent acts, whose members describe themselves as 'Christian soldiers preparing for the arrival and battle with the anti-Christ'? How many have heard of the Army of God (AOG), a Christian terrorist anti-abortion organisation that approves the use of force to combat abortion in the United States, and that is associated with a great number of assassinations of abortion providers? How many have heard of the Jewish terrorist groups, such as the Gush Emunim Underground and the Brit HaKanaim organisations?

Again, many have heard of Saudi Osama Bin Laden and Egyptian Ayman Al Zawahiri, but until very recently how many had heard of Ugandan Joseph Kony, the head of the Lord's Resistance Army (LRA), a group engaged in a violent campaign to establish theocratic government based on the Ten Commandments? How many were aware of the extreme atrocities that the LRA committed, and is still committing to this day, against civilians, including killings, mutilations, rape and in some accounts even cannibalism, not to mention abducting and forcing an estimated 66,000 children to fight for them, all in the name of Christianity? How many have heard of John Earl, a Catholic priest who drove his car into an abortion clinic and pulled out an axe before being shot at by a security guard? How many have heard of the radical Jews who committed acts of terrorism in the name of their religion, like Baruch Goldstein and Yaakov Teitel?

The American academic Jack Nelson-Pallmeyer justly writes: 'Judaism, Christianity and Islam will continue to contribute to the destruction of the world until and unless each challenges violence in sacred texts and until each affirms a nonviolent power of God.'

When I hear some feminist activists speak today about 'Islamic feminism', I feel depressed by this obvious oxymoron. When will we stop compromising and attempting to achieve real change from within the 'rotten fruit'? When will we admit that there is no harmony possible between monotheist teachings (as they are to this day) and women's dignity and rights?

Again, the West usually singles out Islam on its women's rights black record, but it often forgets – and we do too – that in Judaism (according to the Talmud), it's 'a thousand times better to burn a Torah than to give it to a woman'; and that the tenth commandment states: 'You shall not covet your neighbour's wife, or male or female slave, or ox, or donkey, or anything that *belongs* to your neighbour.'

The West also forgets, and we do too, that in The Epistles of St Paul, women are banned from speaking in public and intervening in meetings, and that Jesus Christ did not pick a single woman to be one his twelve disciples. There were mainly two types of women in the New Testament: the whore/sinner and the virgin/pious. The same phallocentric way of dividing the world into black and white, good and bad, etc.

Not only that, but to this very day the Catholic Pope continues to condemn contraception. And it does not matter if 98 per cent of Catholic women in developed countries use birth control pills. What matters is the perpetuation of denial; we need to keep on pretending to believe that every time a man penetrates a woman, the Holy Spirit is there hovering above them (what a kinky voyeur that would make God); and that sex is a 'sacred' practice invented only for procreation purposes. Based on this logic, I should have had sex only twice so far. Catholics, behold your factory of frustrations called the Vatican.

Furthermore, to this very day, the Pope is hanging on to the masculinity of the patriarchal church: beware any woman who approaches this institution, in whatever ecumenical context, and beware that she has any real authority or influence within it. Power is for the origin, not for the 'rib'. And the golden caps of the bishops are too heavy for women's heads.

On this topic, it caught my attention that some fifty clergy-men from the Church of England had decided in early 2011 to leave the Anglican Church and become Catholics because the former announced that it would allow women to be ordained as bishops. The story created a storm of controversy and criticism within both churches. What concerned me in the matter was its obvious discriminatory implications: one of the Vatican's spokes-men, Federico Lombardi, assured that the Vatican puts attempts at ordaining women among the 'most serious crimes', alongside paedophilia. How can a woman with dignity read something like that and not bristle with anger?

And what about the Italian Monsignor Arduino Bertoldo, who claimed recently that if women are raped, it is their fault, because they are tempting their aggressors? Next thing we'll hear that Catholic women should wear burqas too, to protect men from their attractiveness. This while the scandals of the paedo-philic, child raping priests have become a worldwide saga.

Is Judaism any better? Obviously not. Yet I won't allow myself to explore the issue thoroughly, since it hasn't been a direct constituent of my upbringing as is the case with Catholicism and Islam. But I know for a fact that there is continuous discrimination against women by Ultra Orthodox Jews in a country that falsely claims to be the 'only democracy in the Middle East'. First of all, there is no such thing as a democracy in the Middle East. Secondly, the incessant horror perpetrated by the Israeli state against the Palestinians should by itself deny it any claim to democracy.

I will not delve more into examples and interrogations. They are too numerous to be listed, and this is not the purpose of this book anyway. But in order to be more direct, even at the cost of trivialising things, I proclaim: as long as it is forbidden for a woman to be head of the Catholic Church, then I will continue to expose the misogyny of the Catholic Church. As long as Muslim men don't wear burqas as well, then I will continue to decry the burqa as a tool of oppression and discrimination against women, and a humiliating clampdown on their existence. And nobody dare say that these ideas of mine are a result of a 'Western' virus I picked up (which is the easiest accusation thrown in the face of any Arab defending secularism, freedom, women's equality, etc). Human rights are universal, *not* a Western monopoly. And it is degrading to us Arabs to see them as a Western exclusivity. Go back to the Universal Declaration that most Arab countries have (theoretically) embraced and you'll see what I mean.

Women's liberation worldwide has always happened in a secular context, and it is important – and vital – to remember that. Of course, secularism is not the sole guarantor of gender equality. In France, for example, the law separating church and state goes back to 1905. But French women only won the right to vote forty years after that law was passed. And French women's salaries to this day are 25 per cent less than men's. Therefore secularism is not enough by itself; it is a necessary, albeit not sufficient, condition for achieving equality.

How can we fulfil that condition in our complex Arab countries, where in most cases there is no separation between religion and state? I don't pretend to have an answer. These words of mine only aim to decry the adverse circumstances we are living in. But it is a question that we all need to ask ourselves, and try to solve through intellectual effort, and social, legal and political activism.

Let us start by yearning for the free, secular civil societies that we deserve, and work to achieve them, away from the monotheist brainwashing that we are subjected to. Then, and only then, can we begin to speak about a real positive change in the Arab world.

Not one minute sooner.

5

The disastrous invention of the original sin

Show me a woman who doesn't feel guilty
and I'll show you a man.
Erica Jong

The poem
All over again

I am tired of being a good girl.
Be my forbidden apple.
Let me plant my teeth in your thighs
let your blood run all over my chin
so I can be banned
once more
from Paradise.

I am tired of being a bad girl.
Take my luscious hips
take my moist lips
and give me back that last moment of innocence
just before the original sin
so we can do it
all over again
as if for the first time.

The rant
Politically incorrect questions

> I don't need a bedroom to prove my womanliness.
> I can convey just as much sex appeal picking
> apples off a tree or standing in the rain.
> *Audrey Hepburn*

When will a woman approaching a man stop being considered sluttish, while a man approaching a woman is simply considered 'self-confident'?

When will a woman who loves sex stop being called a nymphomaniac, while a man who loves sex is simply called 'virile'?

When will a woman cheating on a man stop being judged as dissolute, while a man cheating on a woman is simply justified by his 'polygamous genes'?

When will a woman dressed sexily stop being deemed as provocative (thus inviting harassment or even rape), while a man dressed sexily is simply deemed 'stylish'?

When will a fifty-year-old woman dating a twenty-five-year-old man stop being criticised as pathetic, while a fifty-year-old man dating a twenty-five-year-old woman is simply 'well-maintained'?

When will a successful woman stop being accused of sleeping her way up, while a successful man is simply bright and 'achieved'?

When will a single forty-year-old woman stop being depicted as a distressed spinster, while a single forty-year-old man is portrayed as an 'eligible bachelor'?

When will a woman who sexually harasses a man stop being estimated crazy, while a man sexually harassing a woman is simply 'weak-willed'?

When will a woman who enjoys watching male strippers and porn stop being seen as an oddity, while a man who enjoys watching female strippers and porn is seen as 'the norm'?

When will a woman checking out a man's arse stop being described as offensive, while a man checking out a woman's arse is described as an 'admirer of beauty'?

And the last, most important question of all:
When will we stop asking ourselves such questions?

The narrative
The bad, the evil and the ugly

> – Is sex dirty?
> – Only if it's done right.
> *Woody Allen*

Our neighbour was a public flasher. He was old, craggy and disgusting, and whenever he met me on the stairs, coming back from school, he used to open his robe (he was always in a robe, for some mysterious reason) and show me his wrinkled penis. 'Come on, touch it. You know you want to,' he used to tell me repeatedly before I ran away and disappeared into our house. That was the first penis I ever saw in my life. Not the greatest of introductions to the anatomy of men, or the most appealing to a child. The device was ugly and the situation was squalid. That must be the reason why, when I became sexually active, I used to shut my eyes firmly whenever I was with a naked man. I wanted to avoid that sight at any cost. Feel but not see. It was a plain survival instinct: 'Avoid the disappointment and the nausea, woman.' I couldn't even get myself to touch *it* with my hand. It simply revolted me. And it took me a long time and a lot of courage, to stare into the 'eye of the bull' one day. But when I finally did, I discovered it wasn't so hideous after all. Quite the contrary.

I caught my parents making love one night. I am sure many children have undergone the same experience, and it is quite confusing, to say the least. He was lying on his back, she was on top of him, and they were covered with the bed sheets (thank goodness). It was merely a glimpse, for I quickly returned to my room, embarrassed and perturbed, as if I'd known I'd seen something I wasn't supposed to see. 'Nailed in the act.' I did not quite understand what I'd seen, but I did not like it. It made me feel uneasy and repulsed. It also made me appreciate and even long for my parents' fights, which had made me suffer intensely before. In my head, them arguing in the evening meant they wouldn't be doing *that* later. What a relief.

Was it my conservative environment? Was it all the 'no-no's that I had to face as a kid growing up in an Arab society? Was it the fact that my parents never spoke openly in front of me about anything? Was it that they forbade me from watching any TV show where two people were likely to kiss? The 'other sex' had always been linked in my perception – and imagination – to the idea of 'immorality' (the famous original sin), and along with that link came the self-flagellating idea that I had to suffer in order to 'pay' for any affinity I felt for men.

Indeed, this is what most of us have been told and taught from a young age: 'Sex is a sin. Sex is bad. Sex is evil.' And some might even add: 'Sex is ugly.'

Yes. This is how the vast majority is educated in the Arab world still, in our so-called twenty-first century. And I know that when I say 'vast majority', I am not risking any generalising misconception.

Not only is sex a sin, it is the 'original sin', and thus the biggest, most wicked of all, at least if we believe the literature promoted by the three monotheist religions. It doesn't matter if it is the reason why humankind exists – most cannot afford the luxury of an 'immaculate conception' – we still have to consider it the foundation of all vice; we still need to believe that God would have invented another less 'scandalous' way for man and woman to procreate, had it not been for that mischievous Eve. For who is the main responsible party for that appalling depravity? The woman, of course. The dissolute apple picker.

So sex is bad, evil, ugly. And it is far worse, far more evil and far more ugly where women and, in our case, Arab women are concerned. Which brings us to the quantity of double standards in the Arab world. Needless to say, it would be practically impossible to address all the symptoms and evidence of this ongoing Arab 'sexual hypocrisy syndrome'. But I will try to configure three of its main products:

My first argument will be the continuing horrific practice of 'honour killings'. Let me introduce you to Maha. Maha was a twenty-four-year-old Jordanian girl who committed the 'crime' of becoming pregnant after she was raped by her neighbour. She was therefore killed by her brother for the shame that she brought on the family. She was stabbed repeatedly in the face, neck and back as well as being hacked up with a meat cleaver. The culprit neighbour denied and relocated, and the Jordanian court sentenced the brother to six months in prison, justifying the light sentence by the 'state of fury' that caused the brother to act in an irrational way while defending the family's 'honour'. The same court also said that the woman's 'shameful behaviour' deviated from the traditions of Jordanian society and stained her family's reputation.

In fact, Jordanian law gives men a reduced punishment for killing a female relative if she has brought dishonour to the family. This has twice been put forward for abolition by the government, but was retained by the lower house of the Parliament (controlled by Islamists). So, in short, if a woman dares to have sex out of wedlock, whether she asks for it or it's been violently imposed on her (like the case of Maha), she has to die. But if a man kills his sister, he gets six months in prison.

Is the problem restricted to Jordan? We wish. The United Nations Population Fund estimates that as many as 5,000 women and girls a year are slain by members of their own families in honour killings. But many women's organisations in the Middle East suspect there are at least four times as many victims.

Obviously honour killings apply to women but not to men. Have you ever heard of an Arab woman slashing the throat of her brother because he had sex without being married? Another, more relevant, and painful, question: do the mothers of the victims act to prevent the crimes, instead of observing a shameful silence in the best-case scenario? (Often they even take the side of the men of the family.) Let's leave it at that. Some questions need not be answered.

Now let's move on to my second argument: virginity. Many Arab women are still expected to be virgins until they get married. If we were living in a normal world this would seem like a tasteless joke. But it is not. Not in an Arab region where there is an overwhelming focus on female chastity and on girls' morally uncompromised manners and behaviour. Not in an Arab world where men are supposed to collect sexual experiences (the more, the better, obviously), but where most women must wait patiently for the ultimate blessed conqueror to whom they will 'donate' their immaculate vaginas (which brings many women to practise sodomy before marriage: 'virgins' indeed). Not in an Arab world where the notion of honour is tied up with what's between a woman's legs, and where women's bodies are considered manly acquisitions. Not in an Arab world where women are supposed to be unearthly immaterial beings that, somehow, are born without sexual needs, impulses or fantasies.

So where does that lead to? Among other things, to hymen reconstruction, of course. A practice that is widely appreciated in Lebanon and other Arab countries. Or to the use of artificial hymens, like the ones from China that almost caused a diplomatic incident between China and Egypt. In fact, the commercialisation in the Egyptian market of the plastic $30 hymen, which allows women to fake sexual purity on their wedding night, provoked the anger of many religious Egyptian figures, who asked for the banning of the product, and considered it a mutilation of the Arab values and traditions.

But what is really painful in all this, at least to me, is how women are accepting this humiliation, and compromising on their right to use their bodies as they choose. Many young brides are even dragged by their own mothers to the gynaecologist, in order to fabricate the lie.

When will these women start asking themselves: Why can men use their ding-dongs freely in the Arab world, while we are supposed to stay 'pure' (i.e. unfucked)? If the answer is 'because women should treat their bodies with respect' (implying that sex is disrespectful), then why don't men do that as well and show us how they would handle sexual frustration? Plus, who says men are better in making decisions concerning their bodies than women?

A subsequent (and rather cynical) question: why don't enlightened parents start giving their baby girls a defloration procedure as soon as these are born, right there in the hospital, just like many of them give their baby boys a circumcision procedure? Wouldn't that solve once and for all the absurd myth of virginity, and liberate women from the unbearable weight of this valued 'flower' that needs to be saved from 'shame and dishonour'? Wouldn't that put things into perspective and help people see the hymen as it really is: a useless membrane, and not a precious gift to that one special guy? Wouldn't that rid us of the ridiculous Arab saying: 'A woman's honour is like a match: it can only be lit once'?

I repeat: if we were living in a normal world, this should seem like a tasteless joke. But you won't see me laughing anytime soon.

Now let me tackle the final element I will address in this chapter: female genital mutilation.

About 8,000 women undergo genital mutilation daily and are thus deprived of their right to sexual pleasure (97 per cent of women in Egypt are subjected to this atrocity. As for the general number affected in the world, it is about 140 million women and girls). This horrifying practice is supposed to ensure pre-marital virginity, inhibit extra-marital sex, and 'cure' masturbation and nymphomania, because it reduces women's libido. Thus, it is used to control women's sexuality (and to divide women in two groups, as per the patriarchal standard: the sluts and the chaste). In fact, in certain societies, women who have not had the procedure are regarded as too unclean to handle food and water, and some groups see the clitoris as 'dangerous', capable of killing a man if his penis touches it. Despite all this, my calendar insists on telling me that we are living in the twenty-first century …

Besides the fact that female excision represents a direct violation of human rights, it also involves many health risks, which include recurrent urinary and vaginal infections, chronic pain and obstetrical complications. But what's most outrageous about it is that, again, same as with honour crimes and hymen reconstruction, support for the practice often comes from women themselves; it is the mothers who drag their daughters, usually without their prior consent, to undergo the operation, frequently in unsanitary conditions.

Indeed, what makes matters worse is that some women dare to claim that being treated with such condescension (being request-ed to stay virgins, undergoing genital mutilation, getting married at fourteen, being buried under burqas, etc.) is their 'choice'. It could be, if by choice they mean 'denial' or 'being brainwashed'. For how could you choose such an insolent, offensive, humiliat-ing way to treat your female identity and body? And how can you talk about choice when you don't have an alternative? Or when the alternative is being ostracised, or beaten up, or lashed publicly, or jailed, or even killed? Do these women really want choice? Then let them choose their dignity.

But let's not move the knife in the wound. It is already wide open and oozing blood constantly.

I could go on forever about these topics. I could tell you about the Egyptian women protesters forced by the military to take virginity tests after the revolution (numerous cases of rape have also been reported). Or about how young Egyptian blogger Alia al Mahdi has been charged with 'inciting immorality, debauchery and defamation of religion' for having posted a naked picture of herself as a protest against the recent Salafi ascendence in Egypt, while the same people who charged her later viciously beat a woman protester near Tahrir Square, after having ripped her shirt open and kicked her with full force on her exposed breasts.

I could tell you about Lebanese boxing champion Rola Al Halabi shot in Berlin by her father, because she left home to live with her boyfriend. Or about Saudi high school student Noor, strangled by her older brother because he found out she was chatting with a guy on Facebook. Or about duplicity in dealing with Arab homosexuals' right to sexual choice and freedom. (Note that most Arab straight men find the sight of two gay men kissing 'disgusting', while they proudly claim that they get turned on if they watch two women doing the same. Also note that though it is considered a punishable crime, gay sodomy is a common secret practice in many Arab countries because of sex segregation, and that the law enforcers and public condemners are often the participants too.)

I could also tell you about the fake, show-off values in societies such as Lebanon's, where people refuse to advertise their businesses in an erotic cultural magazine like *Jasad* (Body) because it is too 'daring', while billboards, TV advertisements and music videos all display a highly charged sexuality, and where you can't even see publicity for a fridge without a half-naked woman lying on top of it, supposedly luring you into buying it (needless to say you won't see any half naked man luring you into buying a new couch).

What could women do in such discriminatory circumstances, you ask? Well, in an environment where many are told that their only place is the home, and that their only role is to raise their children, they could start with the basics: inducing their daughters, and sons, to want *more* and *better* in life. All change starts with the desire for change, and education is key in the process. So instead of complaining about their unfair destinies while falling into the same vicious circle when raising the future generation, they could start by educating their children in a way that could lead to a greater respect and understanding of the other sex, and of the body and sexuality, as a substitute for all the terrible, absurd complexes and illnesses that we are still witnessing today.

And what could a man do? He could start by feeling less insecure, and less threatened by a real woman's strength. He could start by listening to women instead of just *looking* at them. He could start by respecting a woman's mind, freedom and capacities, instead of repressing these.

But first and foremost, he should start by believing in *himself* more. Because that's what the patriarchal pattern entails: an enormous lack of self-confidence in men.

Sex, then religion, then power. Power, then sex, then religion. However you flip it, from whatever side you look at it, it is the same sacred, untouchable trinity, and around this trinity taboos buzz like wasps. The trinity is haloed by ignorance, of course, and when one adds frustration, hypocrisy, lies, backwardness and fear, one gets the friendliest environment ever for cultivating psychological diseases and disorders.

Back to the top: sex is not bad. What's bad is our misogynic double standards. sex is not evil. What's evil is our appalling hypocrisy. sex is not ugly. What's ugly is our sexist, futile values. And last but not least: sex is not a sin. It is a basic, beautiful human need and pleasure.

So let's deal with this fraudulent guilt game. And most importantly: let's snap out of it.

6

The disastrous invention of machismo

A man is a god in ruins.
Ralph Waldo Emerson

The poem
Think again

You might think you're the invincible pirate
and I am the looted ship.
But the wicked robber
is the one being ripped.
So check that heart again
as well as your lips,
dear Sir.

You might think you're Big Bad Wolf
and I'm Little Red Riding Hood.
But go sharpen those teeth
before crossing my wood.
For it is my flesh
that's longing for your grind,
dear Sir.

You might think you're inexplicable
and I'm an open book.
But my clarity is a rod
And you're biting on the hook.

So you might want to think again,
dear Sir.

You might think you're the hunter
and I'm the helpless prey.
But the road is circular
in the chase game we play.
So you'd better look behind you,
dear Sir.

You might think you're the sword
and I am the slashed throat.
But I am Salome's tutor,
and you are my scapegoat.
That head on the plate?
It's none other than yours,
– that is: mine –
dear Sir.

The macho's rule book

> Man is defined as a human being and a woman as a female.
> Whenever she behaves as a human being,
> she is said to imitate the male.
> *Simone de Beauvoir*

'Thou shalt not be disobedient.' – the macho father
Meaning: Do as you are told first, think afterwards. And it's even better if you don't think at all.

'Thou shalt not be other than my mom.' – the macho son
Meaning: Your existence is defined by mine. And your only role in life is to feed me, take care of me and serve me.

'Thou shalt not lose your virginity before your wedding.' – the macho boyfriend
Meaning: I have to be the first and the last in your life. When I marry you, I'll own you.

'Thou shalt not participate in the political life of your country.' – the macho politician
Meaning: You are born to comply/follow, while I am born to command/rule.

'Thou shalt not be taken seriously.' – the macho intellectual
Meaning: You exist to listen, not to express opinions.

'Thou shalt not make as much money as a man.' – the macho work colleague
Meaning: You only have a job, while I have a career and ambitions.

'Thou shalt not show your hair in public.' – the macho religious fanatic
Meaning: You are an object of temptation, and it is your responsibility to protect me from my inability to see you as a human being.

'Thou shalt not hide your tits in public.' – the macho pornographer
Meaning: You are an object of temptation, and it is your responsibility to justify my inability to see you as a human being.

'Thou shalt not say what you think.' – the macho censor
Meaning: Just shut up and follow the herd.

'Thou shalt not aspire to other than to marriage.' – the macho social system
Meaning: Your life is worthless until you've found yourself a husband.

'Thou shalt not prefer reading to cooking.' – the macho educator
Meaning: Why get informed and educated, when the road to a man's heart goes through his stomach?

'Thou shalt not enjoy sex.' – the macho uptight community
Meaning: You are devoid of sexual needs. When the time comes and the good husband arrives, you just have to spread your legs open and fake an orgasm to please his ego.

'Thou shalt not write these kinds of politically incorrect books' – every macho I know
… and yet I do. And I always will.

The narrative

Balls come with a price

> Women are taught to apologise for their strengths,
> men for their weaknesses.
>
> *Lois Wyse*

Meet Mr X. He seemed as close to perfect as a man could ever be; the kind of man that your genes would beg you to have a daughter with: educated, accomplished, smart, funny *and* handsome, which doesn't ruin anything. He was self-confident, didn't have an Oedipus complex (most Lebanese mothers are factories for 'Mama's boys') and wasn't frantically possessive. Moreover, he seemed more blown away by my achievements than my looks and supportive of even my most unrealistic ambitions. He had the expression 'the full package' written all over him.

I had been dating him for three weeks, when the news of a horrific crime shook the country. The corpse of a nineteen-year-old girl had been found in a secluded forest. She had been kidnapped, raped, then beaten to death as she was driving back home from a night out with her friends. The news naturally came up in our conversation on that day. Mr X commented: 'That's what happens when parents let their daughters go out at night.'

That's it. Not one word about the rapist criminal. Not one comment about the failure of our security system. To him, the culprit was obvious: the victim herself. Because she 'dared' to go have fun with her friends, like any normal youngster is supposed to do. That fact alone had put her in the category of 'girls with loose ethics', and a 'girl with loose ethics' is, after all, a rape case fully justified. I can't but be outraged by the number of women who are sexually harassed and assaulted every day everywhere, and how it always seems adequate (for the police forces, the media outlets, public opinion, etc.) to discuss what the victim drank, what she was wearing, how she behaved and how many sexual partners she'd had. How she, in short, 'brought it on herself', hence becoming the accused, not the casualty. If that isn't a patriarchal verdict, then what is?

Needless to say that my genes were horrified and sickened by the man's attitude, and immediately retracted the reproduction offer. And that was the end of Mr X. So much for 'the full package'.

Now meet Mr Y. I had come across him during a colloquium organised by an Arab cultural foundation in Vienna. I found myself seated next to him by coincidence during one of the collective dinners and he caught my attention right away. How could he not, when he was talking vibrantly about women's rights and the vital need to restore their equality with men in the Arab world, as well as the urgency of establishing secular systems freed from the pressures of religion? One factor is not to be overlooked in the story: the guy in question was Saudi. 'Wow,' I thought to myself. 'Finally, an enlightened intellectual in the land of backwardness and social retardation.' He was quite an orator, and that night I went to bed more optimistic and hopeful of change than I had ever been my whole life.

But then the next morning came and with it the time to leave. As we all gathered in the lobby area of our hotel, waiting to be picked up and taken to the airport, I saw the 'Saudi Voltaire' getting out of the elevator with a black, shapeless form walking next to him. After some inspection, I realised it was a woman in a burqa. Asking who she was, a fellow participant in the conference told me that she was the guy's wife. Apparently he had kept her in their room for three full days, not allowing her to even come down and have dinner with us.

If Mr Y was Voltaire, then I was indeed his 'Candide'.

Last but not least, meet Mr Z. He is the husband of a colleague of mine and is affiliated with one of God's parties in the 'land of the cedars'. Mr Z's greatest ambition in life, according to his wife, is to become a 'martyr' one day. His boss was proud to have lost a son in a suicide attack and didn't miss an occasion to rave about how heroic it was to blow yourself up for a cause and take other people along with you. So Mr Z has been fed, since his early childhood, the sick logic stating that 'If my invisible man is different from your invisible man then that's a good enough reason for me to hate you, exclude you, and kill you.' The culture and cult of martyrdom in the Arab world is a flourishing industry of machos: puppets who think of themselves as champions. Criminals who are convinced they are Supermen. We have all heard of drug mobs, gambling mobs and money laundering mobs, but the worst of them all are undoubtedly the Allah mobs.

I remember the day I ran into Mr Z at one of the beaches in South Lebanon. I had seen him arriving with his wife (my colleague) and kids (two boys). During that entire day, my coworker sat under the blazing sun in her headscarf, long-sleeved blouse and jeans, while her 'loving' husband was sun tanning in his bathing suit, and her sons were swimming in the pool. You see, virtuous men 'should not be tempted by the sight of female flesh'. That is why their wives, sisters, daughters, etc. need to sweat and asphyxiate and burn: in order to protect men from their appeal. But doesn't that mean that men are animals who cannot control their impulses? And if they are indeed animals who cannot control their impulses, wouldn't it make more sense to put them on a leash, instead of suffocating their women under a cloth?

I was looking at my friend, fuming with rage and thinking: How could this be fair? How could anybody see this and not feel angry or say/do something about it? And yet it seemed perfectly right to her husband (and even to her, which is worse). For what do women represent for these holy gangsters? A nation of servants and bereaved human beings; projects of widowhood, at best; females who should be happy to wait on their husbands – providing them with food, sex and clean laundry – then send them to the '*Shahada*' when the appropriate time comes, because that's the ultimate meaning of dignity for a man: performing jihad in the name of divine righteousness and truth, and being prepared to die for God's sake.

Yet martyrdom is not a strictly Muslim concept, nor a Muslim invention. Its origins go back to Genesis when God put Abraham to the test and commanded him to offer his son Isaac as a sacrifice to prove his loyalty. Then came Jesus, and the way his 'Father' sacrificed him on the cross to absolve humanity and save the world from the weight of sin. The history of monotheism is soaked with blood, violence and cruel, vain immolations. Mr Z is merely a dupe of that millenary education.

I could go on with an endless list of cases of macho mania: like that 'liberal' intellectual who was blaming me for being too uptight in my clothing, and then made a horrific scene at the restaurant where we were dining because he saw his sister coming in wearing a miniskirt. Or that famous leftist novelist who pretends to defend women's emancipation, but doesn't miss an opportunity to sexually harass any female who crosses his way, as if he only wanted her to be liberated so that she would agree to fuck him. Sexual harassment has reached such epidemic levels in the Arab world that it can be listed as an Arab national sport, with no laws to protect women from it. In Egypt alone, 98 per cent of foreign female visitors and 83 per cent of Egyptian women experience sexual harassment. Most women do not report these cases out of fear, shame and self-blame, since they are constantly accused of 'enjoying the attention'.

Then there is that militant journalist who qualified my tirade against honour crimes and child marriages as 'bourgeois'. The tirade in question was actually part of a lecture I had given at the American University in Beirut on the subject of gender discrimination against Arab women, in the framework of a series of conferences on the topic of youth and sexuality in the Arab world. I had 'dared' to focus in my talk on the subject of honour crimes, child marriages and the celebration of virginity, as three out of countless examples of the schizophrenic way that sex and sexual freedom are dealt with in our countries. But the gentleman apparently considered speaking of women's sexual rights in the Arab world as a bourgeois whim. He protested: 'How can you talk about such things when we are drowning in political and economic corruption, and when people are dying in Palestine every single day?'

Perhaps the dear activist missed the fact that the subject of the conference was neither state politics nor the liberation of Palestine, but 'youth and sexuality' in the Arab world. But he was right. I should have stuffed all these subjects into my talk in order to sweep my guilt away and speak about honour crimes with a clear conscience. Of course, putting an end to Israeli crimes in Palestine is a priority. Fighting fraud and injustice are priorities as well. But respecting the rights of women and legitimising them is also a priority. And what is also a priority is getting rid of male chauvinists who mask themselves with proletarian struggles and tell us that the rights of Arab women (sexual, legal, social, political, etc.) are an exotic luxury. The real luxury – one that we can afford no longer – is this kind of discourse and people. That is the actual face of the 'bourgeoisie': deceitful, hypocritical and manipulative.

'It's a man's world, and you men can have it,' Katherine Anne Porter once said. Well I beg (no, I demand) to differ: You can have it 'over my dead body'.

In the same context, let me also tell you about a woman's magazine conceived in 2010 by Al Qaeda. The magazine's name translates as 'The Majestic Woman', and it is published by one of the terrorist organisation's largest media outlets. In its first issue, we read an interview with the wife of a *mujahid*, in which the 'heroine' speaks of her pride and joy at her husband's martyrdom and reduces the role of women to encouraging their husbands to sacrifice themselves. Piling absurdity upon absurdity, the cover bears the image of a woman (or what is presumably a woman under the heavy black cover that represents her) near a subtitle that announces '7 steps towards flawless skin' – the same skin, absurdly, that is not meant to ever see the sun, breathe, or have a centimetre of it exposed to men's predatory eyes.

The magazine describes itself as 'Islamist and feminist'. I am not going to venture again into the glaring contradictions of this description, or into its direct and obvious role in brainwashing women and producing ignorant, suicidal, patriarchal females. Al Qaeda knows all too well that there is nothing more effective and dangerous than a burqa-covered woman: she can move from one place to another without eliciting demands for her identity card, which transforms her into a human bomb walking through the streets unobserved (this security motive alone should incite more countries to follow the example of France in banning the burqa).

One last thing: the magazine claims to be a step towards 'modernity' and the twenty-first century. No need for further comment.

Fact: According to the UN's statistics on violence against women and girls, one in three women worldwide has been beaten, raped or sexually assaulted. Most of this violence takes place within intimate relationships, with husbands or partners as the perpetrators.

Fact: Worldwide, up to 50 per cent of sexual assaults are committed against girls under sixteen.

Fact: The first sexual experience of 30 per cent of women was forced.

Fact: 140 million girls and women in the world are affected by female genital mutilation.

Fact: Over 60 million girls worldwide are child brides.

Fact: 4 million women and girls are trafficked annually. 60 per cent of trafficked women experienced physical and/or sexual violence before being trafficked.

Fact: In Lebanon many domestic workers are abused emotionally, physically or sexually, and have no legal protection – a contemporary form of slavery. A 2008 Human Rights Watch report revealed that between January 2007 and August 2008 at least ninety-five migrant domestic workers died in Lebanon. Of these ninety-five deaths, forty were classified as suicide, while twenty-four were caused by workers falling from high buildings while trying to escape their employers.

Fact: 3 million women and girls are trafficked annually for sexual exploitation.

Fact: An estimated 1 million females enter the sex trade each year.

Fact: One in two women worldwide experiences unwanted sexual advances, physical contact or other forms of sexual harassment at work.

Fact: 90 per cent of harassment cases involve men harassing women.

Fact: Honour killings take the lives of 20,000 women every year. The reasons include engaging in sexual acts outside marriage (including being raped), wanting to terminate or prevent an arranged marriage, desiring to marry by their own choice and dressing in a manner unacceptable to the family or community.

Fact: The cult of machismo (hyper-masculinity) leads to violence – sexual and otherwise. Women are particularly vulnerable to abuse by their partners in societies where there are marked inequalities between men and women, rigid gender roles, cultural norms that support a man's right to sex regardless of a woman's feelings, and weak sanctions against such behaviour. As for what triggers violence in abusive relationships, it includes disobeying or arguing with the man, questioning him about money or girlfriends, not having food ready on time, refusing to have sex, and the man suspecting the woman of infidelity. Women who marry early are more likely to be beaten or threatened, and more likely to believe that their husbands might be justified in beating them.

How many times have we heard, or even used the expression 'boys will be boys'? From infancy, boys are encouraged to take part in rough games, are discouraged from being gentle and caring, and are made fun of and bullied if they are – by other children and even by their own parents at times. All of this promotes the blossoming of aggressive males who attempt to oppress women and dismiss their voices as they get older and become sexually aware adults.

Unfortunately, many women support such negative notions

of masculinity, mainly by celebrating the bad boys and the alpha males around them. Also, many men blame women for 'bringing it on' (harassment, assault, etc.). And how do women bring it on? Mostly by being members of the female gender. You see, we are all 'guilty' of having tits and a vagina: it's a manufacturing defect.

Bullies, gangsters, mobsters, women beaters and sexual abusers: many men are trapped in a vicious circle of violence that derives from a flawed theory of manhood, a parody of the actual meaning of the word. One that interprets masculinity as inherently brutal; one that hijacks its many positive aspects; one that links testosterone with rage and aggressiveness, and reinforces a patriarchal system based on the dominance/subjugation dichotomy. Add to this twisted education the castration imposed by dictatorships and poverty, and Arab men are bound to need scapegoats to avenge their stolen balls: women. Violence begets violence, indeed.

Are these sad facts limited to the Arab world? According to the European Council, one in five European females are victims of a sexual assault at some point in their lives. 98 per cent of their aggressors are male. In the East, there are generations of women who are being effaced and muzzled, eliminated by the forces of darkness, oppression and absolute ignorance. And in the West, there are generations of women who are being objectified and prostituted; transformed into bodies that are mere commodities. Here we have the burqa, there we see meat at the auction. Frankly, I don't know how a woman can be a woman today without being constantly furious at the insults and abuses that affect her, whether these aim to eliminate or exploit her.

Machismo is a fatal plague. The facts proving it are there, and they are harsh and depressing, to say the least. But where is the cure? Where are the solutions to such a global problem?

One important way of getting rid of this cancerous system, and fighting complacency and the disregard of issues affecting women's rights, is to have more women participating in the political lives of their countries. As long as the political power structure remains controlled by men, I see little hope for change in the basic attitudes that so many men have towards women. There are countless machos occupying the political scenes, Arab and Western. Take Lebanon, for example. It has one of the lowest rates of women's political participation, and one of the highest of degrading women. Recently the Lebanese ministry of tourism was unashamed to produce a short film to promote tourism in the country, playing upon tourists' desire for the half-naked bodies of Lebanese girls. In a country where women have hardly any rights, and where patriarchy and sectarianism reign, the government doesn't hesitate to objectify women in order to attract male tourists. What can one say about this level of patriarchy, discrimination, superficiality, inappropriateness and unethical behaviour?

A second efficient method for overcoming, and even neutralising, the subduing and violent effects of machismo is for women to achieve financial independence. I'd even implore them to become *obsessed* with financial independence. You see, machismo was, initially, the product of the 'male hunter' ideal – I feed you = I own you. Machismo was later reinforced by the rib theory put forward by monotheism (the woman is just a tiny part of the masculine whole). So it is most necessary for women to overturn this by invading the workforce and providing for themselves. Although many are indeed doing that, the percentage of self-sufficient women is still very low in the Arab world. Few Arab women are taught the importance of financial independence. Even those who aspire to emancipation and/or hold a college degree, rely frequently on men to fulfil their economic needs, whether it is a new dress, or a piece of jewellery, or a car, or a house.

Obviously, the ongoing discrepancy in salaries between men and women is a major cause of this. But it is not the only cause. The problem is not limited to the opportunities available. It is much worse than that: it is a result of the prevailing mentality. For example, many women I know pursue an education only as a way to attract a 'better', that is (for them), a richer husband. And this state of mind is not restricted to older generations. When I lately accompanied my twelve-year-old son to a birthday party, I overheard one of his classmates telling her friend: 'When I grow up and get married, I will ask my husband to buy me a Porsche.' I went to the girl and told her: 'How much better would it be if you grow up and start working, and buy yourself that Porsche instead?' Obviously, the adolescent was merely trapped in a pattern set by her mother. Resignation is one of the most hereditary diseases on the planet.

Arab women need to learn to be responsible for meeting their needs. Independence comes with a price: hard work. And the day you stop asking your father or brother or husband for money in order to buy something you want or need is the day you can really start to say that you are free.

Think about it: nothing is more intimidating/castrating for a macho than a woman who doesn't need him to cater to her needs. That would hit the roots of machismo and topple the patriarchal institution upside down. Plus, real men should really feel more reassured than threatened by this evolution: is there anything more gratifying than the certainty that a woman needs them for *them*, not for the financial security they can provide?

Another major solution to this fatal misunderstanding could occur by rejecting the black and white categorisation, acknowledging our dual natures, and accepting that both men and women display and encompass 'feminine' and 'masculine' behaviours and traits. I certainly have masculine qualities, yet this doesn't make me less female. Gloria Steinem asserts that, 'the woman a man most fears is the woman within himself'. I would add that the man a woman most ignores is the man within herself. Once we start embracing the 'other' that we hold inside us, this other would cease to be the enemy. And in my humble opinion, despite the certain implicit differences between men and women, their similarities far outweigh their divergences.

This surely doesn't mean cancelling out the differences between men and women. I recently read about an experimental preschool in Sweden called Egalia that practises 'gender neutral' education. For example, its staff avoids using words like him or her, and addresses the kids as 'friends' rather than girls and boys. Now as much as I am against gender stereotypes and societal standards that expect girls to be girlie and nice, and boys to be manly and rough, I can only be sceptical about such an education's ability to engineer real equality between the sexes. The aim of the school is noble, but the means are not convincing. Our gender is an intrinsic part of our identity: is it not confusing for a young child to blur gender boundaries? Equality should be about everyone being treated fairly and equally, not about forcing everyone to be the same. Equality should be about embracing diversity and respecting each person's differences, not about ignoring them. I resent being told that the only way I can be 'equal' is by denying my gender. Denying someone their gender is inherently sexist, and the words male and female imply a difference but not that one is less than the other.

Another point that deserves to be raised is the fact that the defence of women's issues should not be an exclusively female slogan. The same can be said about the struggle against patriarchy. That is why I have always been troubled by the lack of male participation in initiatives aiming to achieve gender justice and equality; and that is why I have constantly been disturbed by the separation between female needs and male ones, and by other discriminatory practices that create individuals pre-moulded in fear, hatred and resentment of the other sex. Men are necessary and basic partners in the struggle against the injustice women suffer from that emanates from various backwards political, military and religious systems – systems that, just like the mythical hydra, grow new heads whenever old ones are cut off.

The chasm runs deep between the superficial views of femininity and masculinity, and it is hard to fill the gap between them in the absence of a vital fight against the exclusion of the other. A fight like this one requires that the table be overturned – the table of 'men here, women there' – on those around it, in order to promote the universal, tolerant logic of the 'human being' instead.

For this reason, we need a new kind of women: the kind of strugglers who fight tooth and nail for their rights without needing to blackmail or cancel out men; women who don't want to replace patriarchy with matriarchy, but strive for a real partnership with the male gender. We also need a new kind of men: the kind that doesn't require the subjugation of women, the hijacking of their rights and the degradation of their feelings in order to feel 'manly'.

Balls come with a price, indeed. Yet many men don't know what that price is. They don't know that it is about resisting the easy temptation of being machos, and promoting instead a decent, noble and just interpretation of their powers, as well as a liberating and cathartic recognition of their weaknesses. Many don't know, either, what makes a man a man. Some have even reached the point of feeling guilty because they are men, due to all the wrongful associations between masculinity and negativity. That is why it has become necessary, indeed vital, for men to re-evaluate their masculine identity, and to realise that this identity is surely not dependent on machismo, tyranny, violence and possessiveness towards 'the second half of the sky', as Mao Tse-Tung has described us.

What is required now, alongside the female revolution, is no less than a male revolution: a radical, structural, non-violent, non-sloganistic revolution, which can spread a more mature and fulfilling relationship between the two sexes.

And while doing so, gentlemen, simply remember this: Machismo is not about men against women. It is about boys against men.

7

The disastrous invention of the battle of the sexes

I myself have never been able to find out precisely what feminism is: I only know that people call me a feminist whenever I express sentiments that differentiate me from a door-mat or a prostitute.

Rebecca West

The poem
I am a woman[1]

Nobody can guess
what I say when I am silent,
who I see when I close my eyes,
how I am carried away when I am carried away,
what I search for when I stretch out my hands.

Nobody, nobody knows
when I am hungry, when I take a journey,
when I walk and when I am lost.
And nobody knows
that my going is a return
and my return is an abstention;
that my weakness is a mask

---

1   You can listen to the song 'I am a woman' performed by Maria Palatine here: http://www.youtube.com/watch?v=zISgqQeDrzU

and my strength is a mask,
and that what is coming is a tempest.

They think they know.
I let them think so,
and I happen.

They put me in a cage
so that my freedom may be a gift from them,
and I'd have to thank them and obey.
But I am free before them, after them,
with them, without them.
I am free in my oppression, in my defeat.
My prison is what I want.
The key to the prison may be their tongue,
but their tongue is twisted around my desire's fingers,
and my desire they can never command.

I am a woman.
They think they own my freedom.
I let them think so
and I happen.

The rant

He says she says

Can you imagine a world without men?
No crime and lots of happy fat women.
Nicole Hollander

Women have to cook, he says
The only thing I'll cook is your flesh, she says.

Women are creatures from Hell, he says
Good, so you've been warned, she says.

Women can't be trusted, he says
You can thank me later, she says.

Women must obey men, he says
Then get down on your knees and order me to get naked, she says.

Women talk too much, he says
Shut up and make love to me, she says.

Women exist to please their lovers, he says
Say please and I'll think about it, she says.

Women fall in love easily, he says
What's your name again? she says.

Women just dream of getting married, he says
Don't hold your breath, she says.

Women are bad drivers, he says
Remember it when I run you over with my car, she says.

Women don't care about size, he says
I hope you're not counting on that, she says.

Women must be spanked when they misbehave, he says
What are you waiting for? she says.

Women should be tied down, he says
Where is the rope? she says.

Women can't stand one-night stands, he says
Tell yourself that when I'm gone tomorrow morning, she says.

Don't expect me to stay for ever, he says
Is that a promise? she says.

The narrative
'Arab Spring', they claim

> Women who pay their own rent
> don't have to be nice.
> *Katherine Dunn*

The first time I came across the expression 'battle of the sexes' was in the early eighties. I had just seen the movie Star Wars, with Harrison Ford and Carrie Fisher, and I thought that the term might be referring to another sci-fi scenario, where sexual organs were substitutes for Luke Skywalker and Princess Leia. It was in fact the title of a book in French (*La Guerre des Sexes*), written by Maryse Choisy and published in 1970, that I had noticed while browsing in one of Beirut's bookshops.

I was intrigued, obviously, so I opened the volume and tried reading a few pages, only to discover that it related more to Simone de Beauvoir than to George Lucas. But feminist writers were too tough a read for a twelve-year-old girl who had more interest in the sordid than in ideologies.

Then came the movie *Grease* with John Travolta and Olivia Newton John. I was fifteen when I watched it and the only messages that stuck to my mind back then were: 'good is dull', 'bad is good', 'bad is sexy' and 'bad is desirable'. So I wanted to be bad, badly. I insisted that my mother buy me a leather jacket, but the plan failed miserably: a girl with a nose buried in books and a propensity for intellectual debate is bound to scare boys away, even with a black leather jacket on. So it left me feeling even more confused about the hypothetical warfare between males and females. And that is when I came back, fortunately, to the illuminating works of de Beauvoir and others.

Yet the more I read on the subject, the more the theory of the battle of the sexes came to be summed up in my mind as follows:

He drags her out of the cave by her hair; *she* drags him into her cave by his cock, i.e. the insecure man (Superman) feels the need to use authority (physical, economic, political, religious, you name it) to control the woman. And the self-doubting woman (Scheherazade) feels the need to use seduction (compromising with 'stories', blowjobs, social compliance, you name it) to bribe the man into giving her what she is entitled to.

The more I analysed the above, the more I came to think: 'Boring!' Man doesn't need to control Woman. Not at all. Woman doesn't need to bribe Man. Not in the least. This endless game of male power (Macho Ken) vs. female power (Barbie Femme Fatale) had become an outdated kids' game. We needed to move towards a genderless mind power vs. mind power. Soon.

And that's when third-wave feminism came into my life to save the day.

I am often asked about the philosophy of third-wave feminism, to which I subscribe. I usually simplify it like this: Some women cross their legs for the pleasure of men (self-objectifying women). Some women cross men out of their lives (old guard feminists). Third-wave feminist women? Well, they cross abysses, *alongside* men.

Third-wave feminism, which began in the early nineties and continues to the present day (some of its most significant voices being Elle Green, Naomi Wolf and Elisabeth Badinter), persuaded me because it highlighted the variety of women in the world and their uniqueness (beyond stereotyped definitions and binaries). It embraced diversity and change. It redefined women as assertive, powerful and in control of their own sexuality. It fought against typecast portrayals of them in the media as well as the language that had been used to label them. Most importantly, it acknowledged the right of – and the need for – feminism to change with every generation and individual. In fact, in the introduction to their book, *Manifesta*, Jennifer Baumgardner and Amy Richards wrote of the idea of third-wave feminism: 'Being liberated doesn't mean copying what came before but finding one's own way – a way that is genuine to one's own generation.'

Third-wave feminism also recognised important ideas I believed in, such as transgender politics and sex positivism, and avoided the pitfalls of second-wave feminism, which rejected the new currents of sexuality, and tried to tame and domesticate it. Also known as the Women's Liberation Movement, second-wave feminism (which boomed in the sixties and seventies, whereas the first wave refers to a period of feminist activity during the nineteenth and early twentieth century) promoted the eternal dialectical struggle between the two sexes, portraying women uniformly as impotent victims and men as merciless tyrants. But victimising women and demonising men (either due to frustration, paranoia or plain hatred) is a vicious circle, and male domination is not the only culprit in the shortfall: there is also a lack of will by some women to assert their autonomy and/or to leave their 'torturers' before they completely destruct their self-esteem. And women have proven on many occasions to be their own worst enemies.

If it were not the case, how could we explain, for example, the fact that many Western old guard feminists defend today the different types of Islamic veils, including the burqa, and other Islamic repressive practices? They claim they do so in the name of 'cultural relativism', but they'd be better off focusing on the broader picture of human rights 'universalism'. They are defending discrimination, polygamy and female genital mutilation. That frail pretext is also the reason why many Lebanese and Arab feminists constantly attack me and my views. They regard me as the 'adversary', because, among other discrepancies between our viewpoints, I denounce the veil as a discriminative, oppressive imposition: to them, I am merely defending a Westernised view of feminism. As if there was such a thing as 'Arab freedom' vs. 'Western freedom', 'Arab dignity' vs. 'Western dignity', etc. It doesn't matter if I fight for women's free will and choice, and put myself at risk by expressing what many are too scared to express out loud; it doesn't matter if I have paid, and still continue to pay, a high price because of my beliefs and public stands. For those feminists, the struggle can either happen their way or no way. And their way means, for most unfortunately, lecturing others about women's right to be persecuted and discriminated against.

Being a true feminist essentially means aiming at being equal to men (again, not similar to them). And the two things I can't handle or accept about old guard feminism are: turning men into the enemy (I insist: no change in the patriarchal pattern is possible without the partnership and involvement of men) and the rejection of femininity, considering it a sign of weakness; whereas I feel completely powerful in my special identity and its characteristics without the need to adopt masculine standards, behaviours, etc. in order to prove that I am strong (that's a patriarchal trap as well, and a surrender to plain superficial dualities). Men need to be saved from that trap as much as women do. And like I explained in the previous chapter, both women and men have to make an effort to avoid impasse and total alienation from the other sex.

Let us admit it: hardcore machismo is facing a brick wall. Hardcore feminism is facing a brick wall. These are two primary truths that cannot be ignored any more and must be surmounted in order to construct something rational and positive in today's societies. The tense situation between men and women – and to a similar extent between men and their own selves and women and their own selves – has reached the point of barricading behind fortresses of conditioned images, prompting schism, unconscious passive-aggression and a hostile and presumptive attitude towards each other.

But it is no longer acceptable to allow extremist attitudes and practices to rule our lives: such ideologies contain essential insults to the diversity of humankind, insults that tragically impact upon human relations. When a man cloaks himself with macho thoughts and practices, he is not only antagonistic towards women; he is antagonistic against himself in particular. The same thing can be said about radical 'feministas'. These two positions run along parallel courses and cannot meet in any place. They continue their parallel trajectories, taking with them all the energy and dynamism that could be produced by an unprejudiced creative encounter between men and women. They are two positions condemned to bitterness, to disappointment and to deadlock.

Obviously, I am not denying the huge and important gains of the feminism of the sixties. I am a woman who owes a lot to feminism. Without those courageous warriors, without their struggles and thoughts and writings, I wouldn't be the person that I am now. Without them, the world today would be an even more miserable, crappy place. And I am certainly not generalising about them either, for I know very well that not all second-wave feminists are 'man haters'. All I am saying is: 'Thank you, but we have the right to do things differently, now that you have paved the way.' Especially here, in the Arab world, where feminism is still a fetus in many countries.

So is it possible, in the Arab region, to transcend the curse of classical hostile feminism and jump into third-wave feminism, without getting burned in the process? I think so. It is sufficient to avoid the mistakes that others have fallen into and that we can do without. Let us begin from scratch and fight against all fanatic, excluding forms of gender defence, which cause women and men to reject the other and close in on themselves and on limited gender definitions. Let us gather under the ceiling of this refusal, men and women, together at the same time.

My feeling is that the 'fight' between men and women, and all the manifestations of that 'fight', boil down to one word: control. Men control with their brawn and ability to bring food and material stuff to the relationship; women with their sexual bait and ability to say no and withhold emotional and sexual comfort from the little boy inside every man. When this fight/control dance takes the form of a great tango/fuck, it is wonderful and exhilarating. But when it takes the form of a man beating a woman, or a woman verbally and emotionally abusing a man (aka ball-cutting him), it is murderous to the spirit as well as the body. And the circle remains unbroken.

Battle of the sexes, you say? Isn't it about time we call it a tie and start challenging ourselves instead?

We need to admit that the battle of the sexes is also a result of various gender conditioning practices that are imposed on us, men and women, from an early age, and that continue to be imposed on us via subliminal messages during adulthood. If only it stopped at girls having to wear pink and playing with dolls, and boys having to wear blue and playing with guns – we should be so lucky. The twofold formulas, which reject important sexual nuances and the ambiguity of gender (queer identities and atypical sexual orientations), are sadly endless.

Beyond the catastrophic categorisation of individuals as heterosexuals or homosexuals (the dominant heterosexual is seen as legitimate and normal, while the marginal homosexual is seen as 'deviant') and all the meaningless branding that comes with such a categorisation, an example of the dangerous differentiation that brainwashes us is the formula of the *male provider/female recipient*. Indeed, since the day man made fire and killed the deer, and woman took the game from him and went on cooking the meat, we have fallen into the trap of 'he supplies, she consumes'.

A second example of this forced view of 'femininity' and 'masculinity' is the formula of the *male seeker/female prey*: I mean the way many women still conceive of themselves as sexual 'givers' and men as sexual 'takers'. There is no giver and taker in sex: both are givers and takers at the same time. One famous expression in Arabic describing a woman having sex with a man is 'she surrendered to him'. But doesn't 'he surrender to her' as well? Doesn't she gain out of the act as much as he does?

This of course brings us back to the issue of women not being (and not seeing themselves as being) in possession of their bodies. We should resent the 'hard to get' scheme and refuse to conceive of our bodies as a prize. We shouldn't be playing games in order to attract someone's attention. If we don't attract his or her attention just by being 'who we are', then what's the point? If a man needs a woman to 'plot' in order to be seduced by her, then he's weak, superficial, pathetic and not worth her time. And vice versa.

Enough with this nonsense. Enough with the plans and negotiating over yourself with others and tricking them into falling for you. We shouldn't be content to be carried away by the river. We have to *swim* it. Plus, I am a challenge because I am who I am, not because I need to be 'convinced' or 'convincing' in some stupid game. I am a challenge because I need to be conquered day after day, not just on the first day. I am a challenge because, if it's hard to get me, it's even harder to keep me.

The whole thing is, again, a patriarchal plot: woman has to be the 'aim of desire', man has to be the 'assessor', the 'client', the 'buyer'. So she should be good at 'selling' or even 'overselling' herself (the Scheherazade syndrome, again) … This way she appeases his 'conquistador' disorder and gets what she wants. Two birds, one stone.

But wanting without hunting is just another form of giving up. And real hunters don't need spears (physical force). All you have to do is stand there and look the bull in the eyes. Because hunting is facing your fear of what you want. Until your fear lowers its gaze first.

Again, we are, men and women both, hunters; and both hunted. And if we really like someone, then we should be self-confident enough to show it. If that someone doesn't appreciate it, takes us for granted and is just another superficial person who needs the illusion of 'the no meaning yes' in order to deploy his/ her attention, then the hell with him/her.

Unfortunately, in most cases, when you do send him/her to hell, he/she will finally realise how much he/she wants you and start chasing you. But by then it should be too late.

A third significant example of this conditioned view of men and women, by men and women themselves, is the *male subject/ female object* formula, concretised, among other behavioural and self-conception practices, by the historical fascination that most women have about being a creator's 'muse'.

The way I see it, it is just another mode of viewing the woman as the 'material' instead of the 'player'. As if she exists solely to inspire and to be told. Not to articulate and convey. It's a hijacking of her creative voice: a very serious crime (in some cases it is plain suicide on the part of the woman) hidden under the glorification of her role as 'the wind beneath the wings'. But enough with the wind. Time to be the wings.

I don't mind stimulating others. Quite the contrary. I love finding myself in a poem or a painting or a piece of music. But that is not what defines me. I am first and foremost a creator myself.

My muses? Well, many of them are hairy and have penises. So, how does it feel to be inside the crystal ball, gentlemen? Your turn: come on, come on, get up and inspire *us*.

At this point comes the time to talk about the 'Arab Spring', and whether it consists of a real spring for Arab women.

I remember that at the beginning of the revolutions that took over the Arab world in early 2011, United Nations Secretary-General Ban Ki Moon called on the Arab woman to take advantage of the winds of change blowing through the Middle East and North Africa to bolster her rights; in a statement issued by the United Nations' media centre, he declared that the revolutions in Tunisia and Egypt were a big opportunity for promoting democracy and human rights, and that if these two revolutions were dealt with properly, they would provide an example and a model for change in the Arab world and outside it. Ban Ki Moon also called upon international powers to offer strong support for women in these two countries.

Perhaps the secretary-general did not really examine the reality before expressing his optimism about the winds of change blowing over the Arab world, a change that is long due in Arab women's kidnapped lives. So let's take a look at some numbers:

The Islamist Ennahda in Tunisia won a landslide victory, getting 89 seats in the 217 seat assembly in the country's first democratic elections after the popular uprising that ousted dictator Zine El Abidine Ben Ali. As for Egypt, the final results in the first post-Mubarak parliamentary elections confirmed an overwhelming victory for Islamist parties. In fact, the Muslim Brotherhood's Freedom and Justice Party (FJP) won the largest number of seats, with the hardline Salafist al-Nour party coming in second. Is the phenomenon restricted to countries where revolutions have occurred? Not at all. Islamists have also recently won elections in countries such as Morocco and Kuwait, and other countries are bound to follow – including Libya, Yemen and elsewhere.

Why are Arabs voting for Islamists now? Mainly because they have managed to convince the oppressed masses, in crucial need of comfort, that they are the most trustworthy political groups in society. This undeserved trust is based on people's common perception that the Islamists are honest, just, reliable, non-corrupt fellow citizens who will guide public life according to core Islamic values. But what kind of modernising revolutions are we talking about if countries are to be ruled according to religious values?

Do not misunderstand me: these words of mine are not the least bit in praise of dictators and dictatorships. Nonetheless, I can't but be concerned about the growing influence of extremist Islam (both in its Sunni and Shia branches) in the Middle East during recent years. I can't but be preoccupied with the fact that this fanatic Islam serves the cause of the extremist right in the West, a West that too often issues laws against Islamists, without complementing these (otherwise justified) laws with the fieldwork of cultural enlightenment and modernisation – a deficiency which only produces more radicals on both sides and reinforces the vicious circle. I can't but be sickened by how the likes of phoney progressive Tariq Ramadan are promoted in the West at the expense of works by real liberal Muslim scholars like Mohammed Arkoun and the late Nasr Hamid Abu Zayd, who defend the establishment of modern secular democracies and the separation of religion and state. I can't but be worried about the destiny of the region, and especially the women of the region, if what comes after the dictator is as bad as a dictator: that is, a backwards fundamentalist regime, based, among other atrocities, on more misogyny, violence, patriarchy, segregation and intolerance towards women.

You see, too often us Arabs are forced to choose between two monsters. And as much as I am thrilled that the monster of dictatorship is falling, I am equally worried about the new monster that is rising and taking power. Getting rid of dictators is crucial, of course. Combating hunger and injustice is crucial, no doubt. Ending corruption and classism is crucial as well. But fighting religious extremism is also crucial. And respecting the rights and dignity of women and legitimising them is crucial too: that is, getting rid of the patriarchal tools and systems that pretend to protect women and that use this so-called protection as a justification of their oppression.

As early as March 2011, when the whole world – especially the West – was immersed in the euphoria of the 'winds of change', I published articles in newspapers such as *Corriere della Sera* (Italy) and *Die Welt* (Germany), expressing my scepticism, due to the great risks for women underlying the apparent events. I was criticised by many at the time as a 'pessimistic owl'. But unfortunately, time has proven me right. However, you won't hear me happily chanting 'I told you so'. I would have loved to have been wrong in my assessment.

We have all seen them, the noble women of Tunisia and Egypt, participating in the demonstrations, calling for the fall of the dictators and contributing to the protests. 'We have seen them,' I say, and it is indeed a verb that needs to be used in the past tense. For where are these women now, as the new systems are being built, and when there is a dire need for their voices and their active involvement in the weaving of the future and its laws and values? What kind of revolutions are these, if women are content to just be pawns mobilised at will, and neglected when life-changing decisions are made? What revolutions are these, I say, if they did not turn the table of patriarchy on the heads of the oppressors, and if they will only bring forth a new form of backwardness – that of religious extremism – to replace the one that has been toppled? Who is the winner in a game where half the population is nothing but a group of silent – and silenced – spectators?

Let me illustrate these doubts of mine with a concrete example: Amnesty International had issued a report stating that many women who protested in Cairo, who participated in the January 25 revolution were beaten, tortured and humiliated, and forced to undergo virginity tests. One famous case is that of Egyptian activist Samira Ibrahim, who was the first to speak out about being subjected to this violation along with six other women at a military prison where they were kept overnight, after being arrested in Tahrir Square. Another case is that of New York-based Egyptian-American journalist Mona Eltahawy, who was beaten and detained in the ministry of the interior in November 2011 amid renewed protests in Tahrir Square. She was held in custody for twelve hours and underwent physical and sexual assault. Her left arm and right hand were fractured.

When I read of the above news, I strongly condemned the atrocities that these and other women were being subjected to, and felt disgusted. But I also watched a report on television in which an Egyptian female lawyer was explaining to a crowd of under-privileged women that 'females were not created to participate in political life'. I don't know how a woman with any degree of dignity could bring herself to make such horrible statements, especially if she is in a powerful position and there are people who look up to her as a role model. I also don't know how a woman can candidate herself to parliamentary elections putting the picture of a flower instead of her own on the campaign posters, which is exactly what happened with many of the al-Nour party candidates in Egypt, while other female candidates opted to put the pictures of their husbands instead. Need I comment?

Consequently, are the revolts that occurred and that are occurring in the Arab world also women's revolutions? In this sense, are they real revolutions? It is certain that the signs are not particularly promising, and that we are still far from being rid of the patriarchal monopolisation of private and public lives.

Let me give an example that illustrates best what I am talking about: we were recently told that Saudi women have finally gained new 'political rights'. But will this really improve the situation of women in a stone-age country that still forbids them from driving a car and punishes them by lashing if they do, or if they leave the house without their faces covered? Will it make a difference in a nation where many women stand against their own rights, as we saw when a group of Saudi female activists harshly criticised the 'disgusting' violation constituted by women driving cars, and claimed that any woman who commits similar acts 'deserves to be spit on and ruthlessly flagellated'? Will it really lead to a better life for women, while they can still be flogged for adultery, and cannot move or travel abroad without the permission of a male guardian? I can't be but wildly sceptical at best.

Under the crooked Arab regimes (those that have fallen and those that undoubtedly will) erected for the most part on the debasement of women and the negation of their rights, I can't help but wonder: when will the woman in the Arab world move from the cry of 'give me my rights' to the scream of 'I will take my rights with my own hands'? When will she trust that these rights of hers are not a luxury, but a key concern? When will she believe that she was not just born to be married, bear children, obey, hide, and serve the men of her family? When will she realise that all talk of democracy is bullshit without the restoration of her equality with men? And that all talk of freedom is bullshit if her civil liberties are not respected? And that all talk of change and modernisation is bullshit, if her situation and position and role are not re-evaluated? When will she become furious over the gross insults that she is subjected to, and which aim at erasing her daily, in all fields? When will she emerge from her cocoon and transform into a fierce butterfly, scratching her way through with her nails? When will she use her thoughts, her voice, her huge potential, instead of just using her ears? When, especially, will she stop participating in the fortification of the patriarchal system, with its stale values?

In short: when will the 'bomb' of the Arab woman explode? I am speaking here of the bomb of her abilities, ambitions, liberty, strength and self-confidence; the bomb of her anger at what is imposed on her, which she often accepts uncritically.

'Arab Spring', they claim? As far as I can see, it is another winter, or a merely 'cosmetic' spring. But then again, there has to be a start somewhere, even if it is a disappointing, flawed start. The same fanatic Muslims that are voted to rule today will not be voted for again if they do a bad job (and they will); this was never the case for dictators like the ones we saw toppled, who were allegedly 'elected' with a smashing 99.99 per cent. Toppling a dictator is the first shy step towards a fulfilling replacement. Yet the replacement cannot possibly turn out perfect from the very beginning, and without experience. And the newly formed democracies that are now choosing the Islamist parties as their representatives in power still have to undergo the horrors of these systems, and go through the hardships of yet another winter – hopefully the last one – before they realise they have committed an error of judgement and start moving to a real positive change. The transition from autocracy to democracy and from authoritarianism to pluralism in the Arab world must inevitably pass through a phase of Islamist rule. Let us consider it a necessary 'purgatory'.

When my book *I Killed Scheherazade: Confessions of an Angry Arab Woman* was first published, many people asked me: 'What makes you the most angry?' And I always answered: 'The fact that there aren't enough angry people out there.' Yes, the world needs more angry, outraged men and women: men and women who truly and firmly believe that their civil rights do not come third or fourth on a to-do list.

Women living in our part of the globe are severely discriminated against in ways that constitute human rights violations: these violations vary from child marriages, to denial of education, limitation of freedom of movement, low social, economic and educational standing, and so on and so forth.

The solution? There's only one. It's not in patching up the wall that we are facing. It's not in hiding its flaws. It is not in wishing it to disappear. It is not in denying its existence. It's not in rounding its corners. It is not in howling before it. It is not in praying for its destruction. Our strength must now prevail on the tools of repression that have been imposed on us in different ways by others and by ourselves. And this change cannot come from compromising with the rotten system, but only by overthrowing it. So it is time to start fighting *against* that negotiator inside of us.

The solution is to destroy. And destroy. And destroy. And re-build again. Men and women together, hand-in-hand. That is the real *battle* we need. That is the real *revolution* we deserve.

8

The disastrous invention of chastity

> I prefer silent vice to ostentatious virtue.
> *Albert Einstein*

The poem
Recipe for the insatiable

First of all I'll peel
that tender spot
on the left side of your neck
where my tears
and your sweat
run to hide.

Then I'll take your lips –
that sugary fence between my hunger and you –
and I'll lick them off slowly
with mine.

Then I'll suck your tongue –
that mouthwatering
archer's bow
crying out my name
like a zesty dart.

Then I'll chew your eyes –
those two intense windows

wide open above
my ripened moans.

Then I'll bite off your fingers –
those spicy torches
wandering on my flesh.

Then I'll drink
three drops of your poisonous milk
to sink my thirst
under yours.

And to finish
I'll open your chest
I'll cut your veins
I'll tear an eighth you
out of your seven ribs
and I'll start eating you
till there is nothing left
till there is no one left
but
the
delicious
maddening
oh so perfect
taste
of my appetite.

The rant
Penis: directions for use

> A gentleman is simply a patient wolf.
> *Winston Churchill*

Dear Mr Man,

Don't worry: this will not be the usual list of clichéd mantras in the vein of 'a woman's pleasure comes before yours'. You have been hammered with that one so often that you must have learnt your lesson by now, to the extent that it haunts you each time you unzip your pants. As a good fair player, I also recognise that your number one anxiety when it comes to sex is that you are the one who is expected to have the stiff, hard, thrusting mechanism ready. I can't even begin to imagine all the denigrating terms connected with the male failure to achieve the proper hardness on demand. That pressure is surely not making it any easier on you.

Furthermore, I'm not going to go through the pre-coital mishaps: the disastrous, over-chewed pick up lines (yes, some men still insist on saying: 'You have a familiar face. Have we met?'), the 'I'm the catch of the century' tactic, the 'playing hard to get' infection (this should be on the STD list), or the 'sad puppy eyes' approach. I will suppose that the deal has already been sealed, and that you're both by now in a 'compromising' situation.

I am no sex therapist: I surely don't know how to cure impotence or premature ejaculation, and I would never pretend that the following manual applies to *all* women. After all, sex is a minefield and a very personalised one indeed. But from my own experience, and that of numerous friends who have shared their fantasies, complaints and secret/frustrated desires with me over the years, I know it does apply to many, if not most. So if you are about to feast on each other, it might be useful to remember some of the subsequent tips:

1 Showing off is *not* an arousal technique. If you're such a stallion, you don't need to talk about it: it makes you look insecure. She'd much rather be pleasantly surprised by your actions, than fed up with your description of them while you are unbuttoning her bra. (Not to mention you can make much better use of your tongue.)

2 If you feel the need to neatly fold your clothes before making love to her, then you are indeed a very 'good boy', but a very bad lover. Sex requires a battleground, not a sterilised operation room.

3 You're not ten any more: don't ask for permission, don't wash your hands seven times, don't make funny faces, and for heaven's sake, don't show gratitude – she is not handing you the keys to the Promised Land. Furthermore, it is up to you to make sure she is not doing you a 'favour': engorge her with satisfaction and she'll be the one thanking you.

4 Don't be fooled by the call of the seemingly open door. You still need to break through it if you don't want it to slam in your face. So strike even if she is apparently weapon free. Plus, you already have a 'sabre' down there: be generous with the low blows. She won't hold it against you.

5 Alternate bites and kisses, caresses and scratches awaken the animal in both of you. Mark well your territory and provoke her into marking hers. Pinch, defy, spank, take, use, order about, titillate, devour … Tell that civilised gentleman in your head to go to hell, and get down to business.

6 Don't just take her as she is. Take her as she might be. See the erotic potential behind the masks of timidity, prudery, taboos, fear, reserve and social/religious considerations.

7   Tell her what you like, be attentive to what she wants, but do not over-teach each other. When needs and expectations are set and seen in advance, the act becomes automated. Anticipate and beat the teacher at her own game.

8   Sugary Prince Charming is out of fashion. Do not abduct her on a white horse: you possess a much more exciting 'ride'.

9   Do not quench her thirst immediately: let her burn.

10   Take her every time as if it were the first time: beginnings can be endless if you have a fine imagination.

11   Take her every time as if it were the last time: it could very well be.

12   Don't just hold her in your arms: squeeze her.

13   If it doesn't feel inevitable, and if you don't feel drawn to each other like magnets, don't do it (unless you like cold soup). Sex cannot be 'casual'. It needs to be intense and passionate, even in a one-night stand.

14   Don't screw in velvet gloves and a necktie. Don't fuck with a knife and a fork, while sporting a sprayed hair-do. Etiquette in bed? Good manners? These are recipes for frigidity. Unleash your kinky demons and let them run wild in the spaces between the two of you.

15   Those words you've been told are bad and shameful? Those naughty words that you've been too shy to even whisper? Well, scream them.

16 Yes she *can* enjoy sex for sex's sake as much as you do. So stop panicking about her wanting you to put a ring on her finger every time she has an orgasm.

17 She is not breastfeeding you. Lick her nipples instead of endlessly sucking on them like a newborn milking his mother.

18 Go slow. Speed kills the hunger, and there's a big difference between a gourmet and a compulsive eater at an open buffet; a successful ambush happens through stealth, not a clamouring invasion.

19 Tease her, then tease her again, then tease her some more: seduction is an art that demands a considerable amount of sly, playful escalation. I'm not talking here about futile foreplay, which is often dull (and only performed out of a sense of obligation because men have been brainwashed about the importance of 'preparing' a woman), but about the exquisite techniques of torment.

20 Penetration is not a synonym for drilling. The 'hole' is already there, remember? So instead of performing the excruciating act of going back and forth like a robot, ravage her softly: advance deeply, stay put inside her for a few seconds, then fully retreat, bit by bit. Time after time, until she is forced to beg you to remain.

21 Unusual positions are nice, until they give her a leg cramp, and become just a tiring, programmed display of your skills. I guarantee you that you don't need to be a Kamasutra connoisseur in order to fulfil her.

22 Why lie? Yes, size does matter, but what matters much more is how you use your equipment. You could be extremely well

endowed without having a clue about how to please a woman; and you could have modest gear and yet be able to satisfy her immeasurably.

23 Her wanting cuddles after sex and you wanting to take a nap is a disastrous post-coital cliché. It might very well be the other way around. So don't feel disoriented (or snubbed) if she falls asleep before you've even thrown away the condom.

24 Don't do anything *for* her out of sheer duty. She'll sense it and it'll ruin her pleasure. You are her partner, not a soldier on some sexual mission. The more you're shamefully enjoying her instead of mechanically focusing on her, the sexier she'll feel and the easier she'll let herself go.

25 Pillow talk should not involve lengthy descriptive monologues about the Champion League, your mom's awesomeness, your chronic diarrhoea or Italian car engines.

26 A sense of humour is sexy because it is a sign of intelligence and because it releases tension (provided it is the smart kind, not the 'your mama is so fat' kind). Thus it is recommended everywhere, *except* in bed: that's the only place where tension need not be relieved. Funny is fine before. Funny is good after. But funny is deadly 'during': that's when you need to be 'mean'. The meanest you can be.

27 If she is emitting that silly female mechanical drone that gets on most men's nerves, it means she is more concerned with your pleasure than hers. It means she is performing, *not* enjoying herself. Remind her that she is feasting on you too, and deprive her of the temptation to fake an orgasm.

28 'Sacred' my arse. Go for the obscene. And disdain the corrosive religious literature about the slut/saint antagonism. Even if she is, or is to be, the mother of your children, she won't be offended by a good (blasphemous) fuck.

29 Oh and one last thing. Keep in mind you're not kneeling down to pray. You are kneeling down to *prey*.

The narrative
Abandon all innocence ye who enter here

> Chastity – the most unnatural of
> all the sexual perversions.
> *Aldous Huxley*

He was Egyptian. And he was married. Neither got in the way of him being a charming and excellent lover. Quite the contrary. He had the hot blood of the great pharaohs, combined with the torrid frustrations naturally induced by marital sex: an explosive cocktail indeed.

The direct descendant of Khufu was peculiar, though. And that is an understatement. The first thing he did after undressing me, whenever we went to a hotel to 'consummate' our illegitimate bond, was to look for the *Ka'aba* arrow on the ceiling of the room: you know, that sign that locates Mecca and indicates to brave, God fearing Muslims in which direction to pray, in order for them to be facing the holy city when they do.

Oh and how he prayed, my Pharaoh. Whenever the time of prayer would come, he'd swiftly get out of our sinful bed, still naked and leaving little drops of sperm behind like an X-rated version of Little Thumb (sperm, by the way, is not a filthy substance – *najas* – in Islam), and perform his ablutions. Then he'd cover the area between his navel and his knees with a Sheraton towel, face the *Qiblah*, and immerse himself in the *Fatihah*. After that he'd come back, have a sip of champagne, and continue the mortal 'task' with a renewed spiritual enthusiasm.

I don't know if he was praying for absolution from what he was doing with me, or asking for strength in order to keep on having those astounding erections. But he seemed quite fervent about it (prayer I mean, but then again, erections too), to the extent that he'd return with a small red bump on his forehead from all the prostrating. Once, when we spent twenty-four hours together, I witnessed him pray the whole five obligatory times.

At the beginning, I used to watch him bewildered, and found the whole scene quite hilarious, in a kinky, subversive kind of way. Thank you, Dr Freud. A Muslim, married man committing adultery and drinking alcohol, yet insisting on performing the daily prayers that his prophet advised him to carry out in order to be guaranteed entry to Paradise. I wasn't worried at all: on the contrary, I was quite sure that my 'devils' would end up getting to him, and that soon enough he'd bow only to my Venus. But the guy was perseverant, to my disappointment. Three months into our affair, he was still as devout as ever. My reaction having degenerated from amusement to irritation, I started looking for a way out before he grew one of those horrendous Salafi beards. Until one day my 'salvation' came from him: he abruptly pulled out of me, as I was about to have a mind-blowing orgasm, because the Maghrib (sunset) prayer was due. And that was it. I had enough of his god getting in the way of my pleasure. Bye Bye Khufu.

I never saw him again, but I still imagine him sometimes, with his impressive apparatus hanging in the air, getting ready for his mantra of 'Allahu Akbar'. A 'chaste' man, that's what he was convinced he was.

As the above story unfolded in my twenties, it felt like déjà-vu. It reminded me of another 'chaste' man I had come to meet many years before, during my school years. His name was Father Hanna, and he was an exceptional Catholic indeed: he mastered the art of mixing religious guidance with molesting teenage girls. He used to accompany us to mandatory spiritual retreats, and give us group counselling about doubt, faith and the thorny road in between. Father Hanna was trusted by everybody: the parents, the teachers, the nuns, and I wouldn't be surprised if he was trusted by the clouds and the sun and the whole galaxy as well. In fact, he had such a divine childlike face and spoke with such a soothing, gentle voice that Beelzebub himself would have fallen under his charm. All he missed was a glowing halo over his head. But apparently he was radioactive elsewhere.

One day, the wannabe saint, who had a sixth sense about 'black sheep', called me in for a private session. Under a massive wooden cross nailed to the wall, he started his conversion technique with a stifling sermon about the weaknesses of humankind and ended it with his blessed sticky hand landing on my thighs. I stormed out of the room disgusted, and that was the end of my already shaken belief in the so-called chastity vow and other Catholic chimeras.

The two examples above cannot be generalised: I am perfectly aware of that, as much as I am aware that there are millions of frustrated Muslims and Catholics out there who do not allow themselves to surrender to the calls of their 'soiled' instincts. But does that make organised religions more credible and viable? More adapted to human nature? Does it grant them an improving impact on our lives? Do the religious prohibitions and laws make us more civilised and human? Allow me to have my reservations, to say the least.

More on the topic of phoney puritans: when I read about Osama Bin Laden's alleged addiction to porn films in the media, I wondered at first whether the story had been made up. But what does it matter if Bin Laden enjoyed porn or not? This does not alter the fact that his type is widespread and increasingly abundant in our Arab societies. By his type I mean a person afflicted with a deep schizoid divide; someone who condemns decadence on one hand and practises intellectual prostitution on the other. Someone who is virtuous in public and debauched underground. Someone who is obsessed with sex, but cannot bring himself to speak about it openly. Someone who lectures on values and chastity, but couldn't be further from them himself. Someone who calls for prayer and salvation from sins, but lets off the pressure of his repressed urges and complexes in places where no one can see or hear him.

How many of these split characters are there in the Arab world today? This is a rhetorical question; I won't bother answering. It would be enough to say that the most Googled word in Arabic is sex. Just like Christopher Hitchens wrote: 'Nothing optional is ever made punishable unless those who do the prohibiting (and exact the fierce punishment) have a repressed desire to participate.'

In our culture, the notions of virtue and abstinence are considered synonyms, as are those of freedom and depravity, especially when it comes to women. A 'liberated' adult woman is often seen as a slut, not as a person who rightfully decides what to do with her own body, whether that means sleeping with one guy, or five, or none. In fact, to most Arabs the definition of a woman is: 'a human being with an angelic nature who dreams of romantic sunsets, eternal love and spectacular food recipes'; while a man is 'a human being with an animalistic nature who seeks adventure and sensual delight, and runs away from life-long commitment as if it were Typhoid fever'.

Whenever I compare the two clichés above, I frankly find myself more inclined towards the latter, despite my obvious female parts: parts with a 'predestined' function that, by traditional accounts, should have protected me from the hedonistic swamp that I apparently live in, and which also should have led me along the straight and narrow path of chastity.

Again, in our culture, women who dare to enjoy sex are described as sick 'nymphos': a clinical term that describes a woman's surrender to her unruly desires (men who behave in the same way are, of course, 'studs'); a denigrating word used with haughty condescension at best. Those who don't say it aloud have the accusation glaring in their eyes. You can sense their objection, their disapproval, and their rejection too. You can almost hear them protesting: 'How can you be like *that*? Have you forgotten that you're a woman? Wake up and snap to your senses. Respectful Arab women don't do *that*. We seek commitment and marriage to men, not sinful pleasures.'

I listen to these condemning voices, from Beirut to Riyadh, from Damascus to Doha. I listen to them, I analyse them, and I can't help but pity them: women brainwashed by centuries of patriarchal manipulation and compulsory denial, who chorus the lines that they have been taught by Arab mothers, Arab fathers, Arab society, and the Arab religious and cultural milieus. Lonely, desiccated women trapped by the old patriarchal feminine ideal that states that a female should not 'gift' her body to a man unless he puts a ring on her finger first. For it is mostly men who decide what is the proper way for women to behave – the correct, respectable, ladylike way – and they consider this dawdling and time-wasting procedure certain proof of a woman's good upbringing and integral ethics.

Now enlighten me, please: what do ethics have to do with how frequently (or not) I use my vagina? Who decided that the normal needs of my body conflict with my moral values? How does my freedom of choice insult my feminine identity? The real insult here is that many women have been led to consider their body a thing, a present. And to believe that their body's only use is to satisfy a man; it is not for giving themselves pleasure. The real insult is that they are persuaded they are not meant to be free with that body, to take liberties with it, to feed its hunger and quench its thirst.

Many of these women would complain: 'But if I behave this way with a man, he'll think I'm a whore, and he'll leave me for another.' Trust me, this is nothing but another cliché. A cliché that is a conspiracy against you: against your rights, against living your life to the full, however you deem suitable. But then again, what if he does abandon you for another? Would he be worth your interest and emotional investment in the first place, if he turns out to be such a macho prick?

'Chastity' then? An 'industry of complexes'. I wonder who is more 'ethical': a naked woman orgasming between the arms of a man she desires/loves, or a man who masturbates while imagining/fantasising about her, then condemns her in public?

And more importantly: who is more 'corrupted'?

9

The disastrous invention of marriage

There is a time for all things – except marriage, my dear.

Thomas Chatterton

The poem
Still

I want to create for us a parallel world
with no mortal worries:
no expectations, no regrets,
no frustrated fantasies;
no secret desires, no survival kits;
no suspicions, and yet no certainties.

A parallel world,
with no babies screaming in the night,
no college fees to worry about;
no silly morning fights
about the cereal running out.

No sad wrinkles around the mouth
no dark circles around the heart;
no tight chains around the neck,
no 'I'm feeling too tired for sex'.

A parallel world,
with no need for lame excuses

for white lies,
for exit tickets
for coward goodbyes.
No need for 'yours forever'
nor for 'no strings attached'.

An impossible world,
as infinite as an unwritten poem
with just you and me
naked in each other's arms
wide open to one another's hunger
like two free palms,
and time suspended around us,
standing still.
As still as a happy picture frame
on an old wooden desk.

Dynamics of a millenary gaffe

> Bigamy is having one spouse too many.
> Monogamy is the same.
> *Oscar Wilde*

Step 1:

From anonymity, you move on to curiosity. There is a spark. No doubt. Some call it the theory of 'two sticks rubbing together are bound to produce heat'. Others, an 'objective coincidence'. Let's keep it simple and avoid over analysis: two unparallel lines have, after all, a certain probability of intersecting at some point. Geometry 101. There is a spark then. 'The seductive call of the unknown', as the romantic poet might say. And the cat is there. Inside of you. And the cat can't help but peek behind the curtain. And the cat is caught. Willingly.

Step 2:

From curiosity, you move on to passion. The elements of the perfect denial ecosystem are displayed: self-delusion, self-indulgence, self-empathy, self-deception … The other party is not to blame: he/she is to be seen as merely a cynical instrument. Made accessible by X (circumstance, destiny, God, whatever the name) at the right time, in the right place. Einstein, of course, knew it all. So you decide to get married, to breed, and to live happily ever after. This is what they taught you to do once you find the right one. 'Fire, fire,' the cavemen would have screamed. But they did not have words, then.

Step 3:

From passion, you move on to hatred. Marriage puts the lights on. Luckily. Even when it's too late: 'better late than never' is an expression that won't grow old. But 'the sooner the better' is, obviously, a superior alternative. Marriage puts the lights on and the scene is, more often than not, quite repulsive, to say the least: flaws, disappointments, frustrations, annoyances, routines, arguments, weaknesses, dirty socks, i.e. the truth. The naked, blunt, unpolished truth. It's the never-ending story of the huge elephant in the living room. But you've somehow managed not to see it before. The moment of self-kindness is long gone.

Step 4:
From hatred, you move on to indifference. And that's when you become really liberated: hatred is an overrated myth. For it is indifference, and indifference alone, that grants you ultimate deliverance from the mirage. You either decide to stay (for the kids' sake, you convince yourself. Or for social norms' sake); or you choose to break free. In both cases, the commitment is gone. And with it, the ghosts of Cinderella and the ideal Prince.

… And the cat in you goes back to wandering around, quite determined not to peek behind that goddamn curtain ever again. Well, let's not exaggerate: not for a while, at least for some. For it is often the victim, not the culprit, who is tempted to return to the scene of the 'crime'.

The narrative
I take thee to be my temporary love

> It takes patience to appreciate 'domestic bliss';
> volatile spirits prefer unhappiness.
> *George Santayana*

I was crying during the whole ceremony. Burning tears were rolling down my young, twenty-year-old cheeks like Niagara Falls, and I could do nothing to stop them.

My mother was sure it was because I was going to miss her, and was congratulating herself on having raised such a sweet, loving daughter. My father, who was against me getting married in the first place, was worrying (rather hoping) that I was not so sure about going ahead with it any more, and he was starting to think about ways to make my escape from the church easier. My husband-to-be was proudly blaming it on the emotion of finally joining our lives together. My future in-laws were assuming it was out of joy because I had landed such a great catch (no comment).

The bishop was convinced that I was moved by Saint Paul's words about 'the husband being the head of a woman' (I hated the guts of that misogynic apostle, and I still do). My bridesmaid was thinking it was because I didn't like the dress she had picked on her own (which I didn't, actually). My fiftyish unmarried aunt was imagining that I was afraid of the nuptial night, and the inevitable loss of my 'purity' that would come with it (frankly, getting rid of that burden could very well have been the only thing I was looking forward to on that 'holy' day).

But now, more than twenty years later, the time has come to admit that the reason for my bitter weeping during my first Catholic wedding service was even more excruciating than most of the above plausible causes: you see, my new, white, high-heeled shoes were hurting my soft, well-pedicured, fresh bride's feet. And that would be the best metaphor to describe what marriage is all about for me: a painful, pricey, yet at times unavoidable choice.

They say necessity is the mother of all invention. I often wonder how true this assumption can be when I think of inventions like cat socks, toilet roll hats, bacon scented cologne ... and marriage. Four things – at least – are wrong with the latter, as it was conceived and as it is still practised in nearly the entire Arab region. Allow me to briefly go through these built-in flaws with you:

Marriage's first problem in the Arab world is that it is controlled by religion: there is still no civil marriage in most Arab countries, including 'modern/let's party till we drop' Lebanon. All marriages are conducted by religious authorities and are only registered by government administrations after having been registered by authorities of approved religions. Nonetheless, the hypocritical Lebanese system recognises civil marriages contracted abroad, and Cyprus has become the number one destination for Lebanese couples who want to avoid a religious matrimony.

The main hitch of a religious marriage – after it being religious of course – is the difficulty of getting divorced, and the biased system that regulates it (biased against women, obviously). A friend of mine once confessed to me that when she was asked why she was seeking a divorce and answered that it was because she caught her husband having sex with his own sister, the Catholic priest at the religious court calmly told her: 'You need to be more patient with him, my dear daughter.' I felt the need to vomit when I heard that story. Other friends reported cases of sexual favours required from them in exchange for expediting their divorce. Not to mention the custody of children that is almost always lost to fathers. If a wife asks for a divorce on the grounds of adultery, she frequently gets a pat on her back and is sent home. If a husband does that, hell's doors open and the witch/bitch is deprived of every right. Your husband is beating you? Relax and don't make such a fuss over it. We even have a proverb to legitimise that and make it desirable: 'A lover's beating is as sweet as raisins,' the Arabs say. I sure would like to stuff as many raisins as possible in those bullies' mouths.

But when did marriage become a religious practice? In most ancient cultures, the concept was originally created to fulfil the man's need for assurance as to the paternity of his children. But it was considered a private, worldly matter. It involved no binding commitment or special ceremony: it was simply a mutual agreement between a man and a woman to regard themselves as 'a couple'. Then the monotheist era arrived, and marriage became a union that needed to be 'consecrated by God': another genius way to be in command of the masses and to organise sexuality, male–female relations, and political, social and economic rights of people.

In Judaism, Christianity and Islam, marriage has come to be viewed as a sacrament, a holy bond commanded by God, and in which He is directly involved. The same God monitors reproduction and any related sexual activities (invisible men can be very busy, you know). Arab children born outside of a religious marriage are, to this very day, known as 'bastards', and they suffer legal disadvantages and social stigma because of their illegitimacy. It was only recently that former Lebanese minister of the interior Ziad Baroud managed to remove that word from the birth certificates of kids born out of wedlock in Lebanon. Yet there is still a long way to go until their social and legal acceptance is achieved. And let's not even talk about the situation in other Arab countries, like Jordan or Saudi Arabia: many women who don't have access to abortion choose to commit suicide if 'that' ever happens to them, because death is easier than living with the shame of bearing a child without being married (even if in many cases, pregnancy is the result of an act of rape by a family member).

I remember when I was participating in a conference in Milan about discrimination and a woman from the audience asked me about the situation of single mothers in Lebanon. I felt like laughing: out of frustration, of course, not amusement. Single mothers? For all I know, they don't exist. There are only two kinds of mothers in Lebanon and in the Arab world in general: the married ones and the 'whores', that is, women who tainted the reputation of their family by becoming pregnant before getting married. And you don't 'see' the latter. They are simply invisible, whispered about at best.

Yet, being a single mother is a dream for quite a number of accomplished women. Marriage seems an unavoidable decision to many only because of the desire to have kids. It is not uncommon for me to hear my unmarried friends talk about how much they would like to have a baby, without necessarily carrying the burden of a marriage commitment. But this dream is a long shot indeed, as much as cohabitation without marriage is. And I am willing to bet that even time travelling will be possible before we start having proud and respected single mothers in the Arab world.

It is also noteworthy that marriage has proven to be quite a lucrative activity for religious institutions and figures. In fact, it has become a huge financial operation and a profitable market not only for caterers and flower shops but for priests and sheikhs too. Dowries and bride prices (*mahr* in Islam) continue to be required today in some environments. The financial arrangements are usually made between the groom (or his family) and the bride's family. These transactions, which look a lot like slave trafficking, are justified as a 'ruse to make divorce more difficult for a man'. But 'I am only staying with you because I cannot afford to leave you' is a sick logic to adopt in order to validate staying together despite the urge to separate. How is a financial impediment supposed to improve the quality of a relationship between two people? How is it supposed to foster love and intimacy? Oh, I forgot, marriage is not about that.

The second thing wrong about marriage in the Arab world is that it is a patriarchal institution, one that promotes male superiority and power over women. In fact, an Arab woman does not acquire 'status' in the eyes of society until she gets married and becomes the wife of someone (note that there is a special title for unmarried women, same as in most other languages – Miss – and no equivalent title for unmarried men). 'Spinsters' are treated with pity and condescension. Not to mention that wives are still expected to do most of the household work, even those who have other jobs. Obviously, monotheism has had a direct role in establishing the patriarchy of that union, in making it an institution of male rule and privilege that entails female subordination: 'Wives, submit to your husbands as to the Lord.' A good wife obeys her husband and is subject to his authority. A good wife endures any sexist oppression (varying from emotional to physical abuse) as a 'natural' thing because of the cultural, economic, political and legal supremacy of the husband. A good wife proudly embraces the name of her husband (after having inherited the name of her father for the first two or three decades of her life). A good wife is expected to take care of the house and children: while the man occupies the public sphere, the woman operates within the private sphere (she is the caregiver, the 'hand that rocks the cradle').

But is it all men's fault? Surely not. One good example to illustrate that is the many Lebanese wives who outsource childcare and household chores (counting on Ethiopians, Sri Lankans, Filipinas, etc.), but refuse at the same time to participate in the money earning process. They request to be treated as equals, yet only want the advantages of equality. And most importantly, they continue to raise their kids in a way that cultivates compulsive dominance, aggression and narcissism in boys, and passivity or passive-aggression in girls, instead of encouraging them towards an equal view of the sexes.

Going back to the link between marriage and patriarchy in the Arab world, do I need to remind you that men in Islam are entitled to up to four wives? Try to tell these men that you'd like to see a Muslim woman with four husbands for a change: it would be an absolute heresy. But then they could talk to you for hours about how Islam respects a woman's rights and dignity, and is all about 'justice' and 'fairness'. The times of the harem are anything but over.

And what about the law that states that a rapist can walk away free if he marries his victim? On this topic, let me tell you the story of Amina Filali, the sixteen-year-old Moroccan girl who killed herself in March 2012 after she was forced to marry her rapist. In fact, article 475 of the Moroccan penal code allows for the kidnapper of a minor to marry his victim to escape prosecution, and it has been used to justify the traditional practice of making a rapist marry his victim to preserve the honour of the woman's family. Amina had complained to her mother that her husband was beating her repeatedly during their five months of marriage, but her mother counselled 'patience'. So the girl ended her life by swallowing rat poison. The sick law mentioned above is not limited to Morocco: in many parts of the Middle East, including Lebanon (article 522 of our penal code is the same, and it even enables child molestation and sexual abuse of mentally handicapped people), there is a law whereby a rapist/aggressor can escape prosecution if he marries his victim, thereby restoring her honour. That is how a criminal is 'saved' while his victim is 'punished' all her life.

And what about *zawaj al mut'ah* or *nikah al mut'ah* (pleasure marriage) in Shia Islam? It is a fixed-term contractual marriage, which is automatically dissolved upon completion of its very short term, with no divorce required. The female simply needs to say: 'I marry myself to you for the specified sum [she mentions the amount] and for the specified time period [she mentions the time period].' Then the man says: 'I accept.' And that's it. A friend of mine told me that his cousin wanted to contract a pleasure marriage with a Russian prostitute once, so he made her repeat like a parrot the Arabic holy words required in order for the marriage to be lawful. Now for a sane human being, this would be considered legalised prostitution, since the so-called marriage can last for as little as half an hour and the woman receives financial compensation for it. But for Shia Muslims, this is considered honest wedlock, not debauchery: just mention the name of Allah and some Qur'anic verse and you're not sinning or fucking a prostitute any more. You're simply consummating a legal marriage legitimised by God. Also, note that the wives in this case are not confined to a maximum of four, since the husband is not required to support the wife and the marriage is not permanent. So a man can have as many 'pleasure wives' as he wishes (and can afford): again, it has the stink of the harem reeking from it.

There is also the *zawaj al misyar* or *nikah al misyar* (travel marriage) mostly practised by Sunnis, whereby a man can take a temporary wife if he travels abroad. In a conservative society that punishes *zina* (fornication) and other sexual relationships established outside a marriage contract, this, again, is institutionalised 'debauchery'. There is much similarity between *mut'ah* and *misyar*, with two exceptions: the pre-fixed date of expiry in *mut'ah* and the fact that the Sunni *misyar* requires two adult male witnesses, whereas in the Shia *mut'ah*, the two witnesses may be just Allah and the Qur'an.

And what about the child brides? Islam teaches that a girl enters adulthood at the beginning of puberty (as if the onset of puberty equals maturity), and thus becomes ready for marriage.

The Islamic source materials state that Mohammed proposed marriage to Aisha when she was six. He assumed her silence constituted her consent. Some two to three years later, he consummated his marriage with her. He was fifty-two and she was nine. Was that horrible practice limited to Mohammed's era? One wishes. The scandalising number of child brides in the world today, girls as young as eleven or twelve, who are sold into marriages from Iran to Yemen and from Saudi Arabia to Afghanistan proves that the problem is far from being solved. The humanitarian organisation CARE estimates that more than 60 million girls under the age of eighteen are married, many to men twice their age or older. Obviously, not all these child brides are Muslims, and I am not suggesting that Islam is the *only* reason for child marriage in the world. Clearly there are other economic, cultural and social issues behind it. But Islam at the very least allows, enables and even encourages the practice of child brides, since the prophet Mohammed is the 'best of examples'. Muslim child brides are also reported to be on the increase in Western countries like the UK and Canada.

One particularly tragic case is that of thirteen-year-old Yemeni child bride Ilham Mahdi al Assi who died in 2010, three days after her wedding, after she was tied down, raped repeatedly and left bleeding to death by her 'loving' husband. Another case is that of ten-year-old Saudi Hala al Youssef who, in August 2009, was returned to her elderly husband by her father. The girl had been hiding with her aunt for over a week when she was discovered. Originally it was her older sister who was betrothed to the eighty-year-old man, but when the elder girl chose instead to further her education, their father gave the ten-year-old to him as a replacement bride, according to Sharia.

If the so-called Sharia isn't institutionalising paedophilia, prostitution and slave trafficking, then what is?

A third flaw in marriage is that it imposes unrealistic expectations on human beings. One example of this is that it is envisaged beforehand as a perpetual contract: there is no expiry date on that ring, there is no way out from that one roof under which you both are required to live, which results in a feeling of suffocation and a huge lack of privacy and breathing space. Of course, there is always the option of living in separate houses (I went for that in my second marriage), but it is economically hard to maintain.

Despite the high and increasing divorce rates everywhere in the world, marriage is still conceived of as a 'till death do us part' institution. But doesn't that kill the thrill of it? Isn't it better to think it might end at any minute? Wouldn't it be more exciting to consider it like an entry visa instead of a permanent residency? After all, it is known that visitors enjoy and appreciate a country more than its citizens. Worries (given and received) are an art form. Nothing compels appreciation more than feeling we could lose someone at any moment: it pushes us to enjoy him/her much more.

According to recent statistics, women initiate separations more often than men. Men are apparently more reluctant to leave. And I can pretend to know why. It is, in my humble opinion, sometimes due to the fact that married men have more access to the freedom of bad behaviour than women i.e. more access to 'getting away with it'. They can have 'good wives' at home, taking care of their kids, providing them with the stability of a durable emotional relationship and with a conventional social framework when they need it; *and* they can do whatever they want outside, if they feel like it. In fact, most statistics indicate that men everywhere are more likely to cheat than women (although the number of female infidelities is rising). But it is not because women are 'less tempted than men', or more 'resistant to sexual attraction', as they are told repeatedly since childhood: it is simply because it is often practically easier for men to do it (they frequently have more freedom of movement and greater access to alibis), and because a man cheating is less socially condemnable than a woman cheating in our patriarchal world – a man having an affair is often excused, while a woman having an affair is judged to be a slut. Extramarital sex when practised by men is just a forgivable slip or a 'fleeting mistake'; while extramarital sex when done by a woman is a serious 'betrayal'. Not to mention the weight of guilt, which is historically much higher on women than on men.

So, in short, men have the luxury of doing everything that looks like leaving their wives, except the actual (annoying) leaving part. Some of them even have a 'green light' from their wives to stray and have escapades every now and then, as long as they are 'discreet' and preserve the sacred facade. They have the best of both worlds, so why the hassle and the headache?

Of course, access to affairs isn't the main reason women initiate separation more than men. The reason women are more likely to leave is less about cheating than it is about their unwillingness to settle. For most men, appearances are crucial. And an 'okay marriage', if it preserves those appearances, is enough. 'Okay' is worth settling for. Most women want more than plain 'okay'. They want passion and intimacy with a partner. The main reason for this is that men and women are still raised with very different attitudes towards marriage. Patriarchal culture imposes a romantic idealistic image of marriage on young girls. Boys, on the other hand, grow up in a guy culture that sees marriage as the end of freedom. So, in short, boys are taught that marriage is about settling down ('boring'), while girls are taught that marriage is about finding enduring happiness ('and they lived happily ever after'). It is obvious who has higher expectations and consequently who is more likely to be disappointed and frustrated.

That is the reason why I advocate marrying two, three or four times as our needs change, even if the price for that is throwing away a relationship rich in history and upsetting our kids' lives. Because in my opinion, our kids' lives can be more upset by bitter fights and arguments, and by our own disappointment, than by a civilised separation.

Too many of us confuse being a good partner with the willingness to go on. Too many of us think that a good person keeps his/her promises, even when those promises are making him/her miserable. A good, fulfilling relationship needs more than a depressing determination not to leave no matter how bad things get; it deserves more than the 'conscience-comforting' pretext of 'staying because of the kids'; it requires more than just cowardly pretending nothing is wrong. It needs and deserves and requires, first and foremost, a profound desire to share your life with someone. But again, marriage is not about that.

One more flaw of marriage is the requirement of lifelong monogamy. Religious laws do not even allow a person to *desire* another man/woman, let alone do *it* with him/her. (Again, the woman being considered the property of her husband, her acts of adultery are always treated with more severity than those of the man.) I know that I am walking in a minefield here, but I do not expect a man to be faithful to me a priori. I don't want a man forcing himself not to sleep with other women while sleeping with me. If a man ever chooses to not sleep with other women, I want it to be unavoidable and inescapable like a fire devouring a forest, not deliberate and rational like a car purchase. I want him to do it because he couldn't do otherwise, not because he is afraid to 'hurt' me, or terrified of being discovered, and surely not out of moral obligation, marriage vows and the pressures of the guilt game.

Faithfulness as a strict ethic, and not as a natural, spontaneous instinct, generates frustration. And I do not want a frustrated man in my life. Frustration demands gratitude. Gratitude requires sparing. Sparing leads to duplicity. Duplicity generates lies. Lies produce disappointment. Disappointment leads to revulsion: an endless vicious circle of unnatural behaviours.

Confusing human decency with monogamy is quite a simplistic cliché. As if the only thing keeping people from behaving like animals is the obligation of being sexually faithful to one partner. How I wish that were true. Monogamy is too often a dogma triggered by the inescapable burden of religion, which teaches everybody to act as a machine, replicating behaviours never to be questioned. But being human means questioning everything, in an open way. Being human means knowing who we are and choosing a path not because we are forced to walk it but because we have paved it. Being human also means accepting the consequences of our actions and choices, not looking around for scapegoats – another religion-driven behaviour.

Monogamy is too often an ownership script, a socially compelled sexual incarceration that can lead to anger and contempt. It is not the only appropriate way to be in a relationship, and it is time that society found other forms of acceptable relationships: one of these could be the sexually open marriage.

You see, I don't believe it is 'infidelity' that breaks up marriages; it is often the unreasonable expectation that a marriage must restrict sex that breaks up a marriage. Emotional intimacy is the real threat to a relationship, not sex. Most people cheat not because they don't love their partner, but simply because they want to have sexual flings with others. They can be emotionally monogamous at the same time as being sexually polygamous. They often stay with their long-term partners for the socio-emotional connections, while craving recreational sex with others from time to time. And controlling one's partner to prevent the latter only makes matters worse: it makes them want to leave, since humans have repeatedly proven to be bad at controlling their bodies' desires and urges.

I'm not advocating cheating here; I'm advocating open and

equitable relationships, beyond patterns of jealousy and scrutiny, which can be very damaging and claustrophobic in a marriage. That is why mutual transparency and honesty are required in an open relationship – to stop the concept from being transformed into a device for deception. It simply makes more sense than lying and cheating. A second important point about the framework of this concept is that *both* partners should be okay with it. Most men want sex on the side for them, but not for their wives. That is unfair, selfish and totally unacceptable: just another patriarchal mould.

Scandalised? Take a minute to ask yourself why. Could it be because you've been conditioned to be so? Could it be because you believe in freedom taken but not in freedom given? Could it be because you've been trained to confuse love and ownership? Could it be because you're scared of 'competition'? Well, guess what: there are always phantoms of others in your bed. A couple having sex is almost never composed of just two people.

I once published a short story about a married woman mentally preparing the grocery list while having sex with her husband. The story raised outrage among some readers, as if I had committed sacrilege. If you want a shot of denial, our countries are the place to get it. But you might want to be careful: the risk of overdosing is quite high.

How many married women 'undergo' marital sex like some kind of a chore? How many do not enjoy the 'Saturday night three minutes in and out' ritual? Some even tell me they are relieved that their men have affairs: less sexual pressure on them and more expensive gifts from the cheating husbands. Yes, even adultery is a financial market. Who is more corrupt though? The bribers or the bribed? Cynically, I'd answer neither: it's simply a matter of supply and demand.

I am not saying there aren't monogamous people out there. Of course there are. And monogamy is beautiful when it is reciprocal and genuine: contradictorily, there is nothing more liberating than the feeling of not wanting, needing or desiring anybody but that one person you are in love with, and him/her wanting, needing and desiring no one else but you. I have been there, and saying that it is intoxicating and wonderful is an understatement. But it has to be shared and instinctive in order for it to function and be meaningful. How many are monogamous out of duty, or fear, or guilt, or lack of opportunity; and how many are monogamous out of real love for the other person? I have a huge respect for the latter, but 'only you' is too often a big fat lie.

I am not pretending that what I am suggesting is easy. Call me a radical, but I only respect, and accept, and believe in the 'I am loyal to you 'cause I can't help but be' kind of faithfulness. Anything less than that is an insult.

Obviously, to list all marriage flaws would prove to be interminable: the routine, the lack of space, the fighting over futile details, the boredom, etc. But you all know those defects, and I am surely not the first to discover that this institution is increasingly becoming obsolete. Instead, allow me to end by suggesting a revisited, less unrealistic and idealised version of the marriage vows:

Old version: I take thee to be my lawfully wedded (husband/wife), to have and to hold. I promise to be true to you in good times and in bad. I will love you all the days of my life, from this day forward, until death do us part.

New version: I take thee to be my (temporary love). I shall gladly hold you when you and I feel like it, but I won't 'have' you and you surely won't 'have' me. I can't promise anything to you, but I'd rather we have good times than bad. I will love you as long as I can, not a day longer. It won't be death to do us part: it will most probably be another man/woman. So do you want to live 'happily ever after' with someone else, or do you want to live on the edge with me?

10

The disastrous invention
of getting old

> He dares to be a fool, and that is the first
> step in the direction of wisdom.
>
> *James Huneke*

The poem
The artichoke theory

The leaves are so hard. You touch them and they feel impenetrable; indestructible. And let's not forget the aggressive thorns. You smile at the artichoke, but it doesn't smile back at you: such an intimidating creature. As if it is warning you: 'Go away. I am too tough for you and you can't handle me.'
But you should know better.

So you start to unwrap it. Day after day, year after year. One leaf at a time, one defensive shield after the other. And every time you think you're finally close to the flesh, more menacing leaves appear. As if it is telling you: 'There is no use. What you see is what you get. Run for your life.'
But you should know better.

So you insist. And you keep on removing the rigid layers of fear, hurt, doubt, disappointment that the artichoke has grown over time in order to protect itself from the fake and the ruthless. Your fingers hurt, your patience almost runs out, but you are too obstinate and too passionate to give up. Because you know that's the only way to deserve what's coming next.

And finally, finally the artichoke rests all naked in your tired incredulous hands. No more thorns, no more spiky leaves: just a soft gentle heart, asking to be eaten. As if it is imploring you: 'Take me. I don't want to fight any more. Your faith in me has earned you my surrender, and has earned me my deliverance.'

And so you eat it. You eat the ripe heart. *Your* ripe heart. And the heart blossoms inside of you. And you feel so proud, because despite all the canned artichoke hearts out there, peeled and ready for you to eat, you chose to have yours the hard way. And you feel so good, because even though the journey of life has been long and difficult, it was worth it.
And you understand that the artichoke is but the metaphor of your maturity; the metaphor of your existence ...
The metaphor of you.

The rant
So what?

A person's maturity consists in having found again
the seriousness one had as a child, at play.
Friedrich Nietzsche

I am 'in my forties' now. Or so I'm notified by my birth certificate. That scary age where women are told they are starting to become *old*; and men, *interesting*. You see, even maturity has a discriminative lexicon.

Yes, I am in my forties now. So what? Sure, I have some wrinkles around my eyes. You see, I have smiled a lot, and I have frowned a lot. I have laughed and I have cried. I have *lived*. But the best is yet to come. My skin is paying the price of my greed? So be it. Because even if I am lonely at this moment, I am less alone than when I had a smooth face. I don't covet the fruits any more. I devour them. Eyes wide open.

I am in my forties now. So what? Sure, I have some grey hairs on my head. You see, I have witnessed a lot of good things, and a lot of bad things. I have fought. I have won. I have lost. My curls are paying the price of my madness? So be it. I don't need to dye my hair to feel younger. The fire of passion inside of me will take care of that. And its redness doesn't turn white.

I am in my forties now. So what? Sure, I look before I leap. But I still leap. Even when there is no one to catch me. I know I will catch myself. I always do. I break a bone or two? So be it. I break someone else's heart or mine? So be it. Wrong turns are the true path to discovery. I don't want to stop travelling towards the unknown. Ever. And my bruised knees are stronger than they seem.

I am in my forties now. So what? Sure, I trust others much less. But I still trust. Even when I am terrified. Because I have learnt that the real loser in life is the deceitful, not the deceived. I get slapped every now and then? I get stabbed in the back from time to time? So be it. I am proud of my open scars. And the more they bleed, the thirstier I become.

I am in my forties now. So what? Sure, I don't believe in many things. But I do believe: I believe in freedom. In love. In friendship. In mystery. In desire. In surprise. In words. In silence. In dignity. In a giving that is more rewarding than taking. And mostly: I believe in Joumana. I am told lies at times? So be it. Cruelty is lying to oneself, not to others. And the punishment is within.

I am in my forties now. So what? A twelve-year-old girl is still playing and giggling inside of me. She doesn't give a damn about wrinkles. About grey hair. About breaking her bones or hurting her heart. She doesn't care about deception, about fear, about slaps and stabs and scars.

She is as light, as careless as a poem that is yet to be written … And she is not planning on growing old any time soon.

We can all be Peter Pan

> To exist is to change, to change is to mature,
> to mature is to go on creating oneself endlessly.
> *Henri Bergson*

Like most kids, my youngest son, Ounsi, loved to draw when he was growing up. He made me beautiful aquarelle paintings, which I kept everywhere: in my bag, under my pillow, between my books and in my travel kit. I hung his colourful abstract productions on the bathroom mirror, on the fridge, in my bedroom and even in my office, right there next to works by great Lebanese painters – the usual mum stuff.

Come sixth grade, though, Ounsi started to resent drawing. The papers he handed me were becoming scarce. Not to mention that he spent the entire first trimester moaning about his 'old' art teacher: 'Our old teacher this; our old teacher that.' 'She just doesn't get me,' he used to repeat over and over again with a sigh. I was totally under the impression that he was some kind of a post-modern genius, the future Andy Warhol of Lebanon, snubbed by an elderly traditionalist mentor who didn't understand the new artistic forms and expressions.

After one too many complaints, I decided to have a meeting with the lady to try to blow some dust off her extinct views on art. That same morning, as I was kissing Ounsi goodbye before he went to class, it occurred to me to ask him: 'How old is your old teacher, exactly?' And the reply came like a kick in my stomach. After a long whistle that meant she belonged more to the Jurassic era than to the twenty-first century, he said: 'Oh, really old. She must be like forty.' I had just turned forty the week before.

That's when it suddenly hit me: in my kids' perception, forty meant I was supposed to knit socks by the fire, while to me it meant wearing fishnet stockings with a nice skirt. To them it meant I would soon need a stick in order to move around, while to me it meant dancing till dawn with my friends. To them it meant 'it was over', while to me it meant 'it is just starting'.

I am undoubtedly stating something self-evident when I say that obsession with youth is a patriarchal invention, as is obsession with plastic beauty and the addiction to aesthetic surgery that derive from it. With airbrushed pictures in magazines representing impossible women, with an industrialised world that places so much importance on appearance (especially a woman's beauty) and with the cult of celebrities, the 'rich and famous' who can afford to buy their youth, there is more pressure than ever to stay young and beautiful. Because the (patriarchal) media makes us believe that only the young and beautiful matter. The (patriarchal) media makes us believe that only the young and beautiful have a bright social life and lots of friends. The (patriarchal) media makes us believe that only the young and beautiful are successful and happy and desirable. That is why many women lie about their age and cry on their birthdays, instead of growing old peacefully and gracefully. That is why many women are investing so much money to halt the ageing process (creams, injections, surgeries, etc.), instead of being proud of their laugh lines and allowing their hair to turn silver.

As we grow older, we are all bound to feel frustrated. We are all bound to feel like we are running out of time. We are all bound to feel like we are being threatened by the tick tock of the clock. How could it not be so, when youth represents infinite possibilities, while maturity's price is a long list of worries and responsibilities? But is that a reason to drown ourselves in a sea of adolescent-level stimulation and escapism? Is that a reason to get lost in the meaning of superficial expressions like 'fifty is the new forty, thirty, twenty, etc.'? Is that a reason to undergo an endless series of face-lifts, lip augmentations, cheek implants and other procedures that alienate our natural appearance?

Take Lebanon; for example: many beautiful, healthy young women who don't need cosmetic surgery are turning to it increasingly. Many even attempt to recreate their own facial structure so that it resembles that of a famous person: that is why you find in the streets and bars of Beirut so many women who look like the caricatured clones of a famous singer, and of themselves. Cosmetic surgery is often not about restoring beauty and youth; it's about counterfeiting them, and it has become a sickness that is spinning out of control as an epidemic; it's psychologically infectious, and it is fooling so many women into thinking they need to let a doctor crush their bones or cut them apart with a knife so that they can attract men's attention. Take a look under the polished hood. I have, and it's not pretty.

It's all about fear, fear of being unworthy and imperfect: a fear that preys upon the insecurities of women all over the world; women who strive to stay frozen in a perpetual adolescence and confuse the quest for youth with the quest for immaturity, all in the name of a lost self-confidence, ruined by patriarchal systems that objectify females and undermine their capacities, reducing them to nice figures and smooth faces.

These last items remind me of a poster I saw recently, on the windows of a famous bookstore chain, showing a naked woman with the words 'the pleasure of culture' spread over her exposed body. So what is pleasure, exactly, for the people behind the concept? A nude woman, obviously. Is that what we women are all about? An endless metaphor for the alluring apple? Haven't we had enough of that by now, whether in the West or in the

East? If I wanted to be cynical, I'd say that I have nothing against the notion, except that I do not find my own needs fulfilled there, being a poor heterosexual attracted to men, and not the least bit turned on by the sight of a woman's tits … So when will all the machos of the advertising business begin to realise that we exist? When will they stop exploiting our arses to sell cars, furniture, drillers and pesticides? If they insist on using the body as an enticement in order to promote their products, they should start putting some male buttocks before our eyes. Do they believe that women are beyond those 'basic instincts'? Well then, that would be an acknowledgement of our superiority, wouldn't it?

It is because of such patriarchal systems that self-assurance became solely based on looks rather than intelligence and talent, and that silicone and botox became miraculous cures for unhappiness and depression. It is because of such patriarchal values that living became a synonym for 'performing'. We seem to have forgotten that only when the idea of an audience fades away, do we become truly alive.

The contradiction, and the injustice, lies most of all in the one way street that this obsession seems to travel on: because when it comes to feelings and seduction, the looks and age of men don't matter for most women. It's the man's brain and attitude and the way he treats a woman that are sexy to her, not his looks. But how many men can say the same about women they are attracted to? How many prefer the mind over the boobs, and the personality over the arse? When will their woman stop being a trophy and start being a partner? And when will men understand that even if they look like Brad Pitt, but act like pricks and don't use their brains, they will never conquer a smart, real woman? While on the other hand, if they are intelligent, self-confident, generous and funny, they can seduce the most beautiful, bright woman on Earth, even if they look like pandas.

'I have accepted fear of change as a part of life. And I have gone ahead despite the pounding in the heart that says: turn back' (Erica Jong). I fear change too, obviously. But at the same time, I am much more fervent about looking ahead than about turning back; much more excited about the future than about the past. That is why I'd much rather *feel* young than look young: the former is not a necessary result of the latter. We can all be Peter Pan from the inside. No scalpel needed for that kind of transformation.

There are so many disastrous inventions in this world. If only they were limited to the ones listed in this book. They are in fact so numerous that at times I ask myself: 'Am I over-equipped or under-equipped for life?' My guess is I'm the latter. One thing is for sure: we're an obvious mismatch. Sometimes, when I look around me, I feel like searching for the spaceship that dropped me here forty-one years ago.

Another certainty I have is that us human beings are construction sites. All of us. But we don't need to decide whether to be a skyscraper or a beach house. A casino or a kids' playground. A strip club or a shelter for the homeless. A train station or a museum. An orphanage or a bridge. A power plant or a toy factory. A bookstore or a lingerie boutique … At least, I wouldn't want to. And until I figure out how to be all of the above at once, I will keep on fighting. Because no matter what you and I have been told, good things do *not* come to those who wait. Good things come to those who get up and take.

Their beautiful voices in my head

But I have promises to keep,
and miles to go before I sleep
and miles to go before I sleep.
Robert Frost

'In principio erat verbum': At the beginning there was a word. A word inside a poem. A word inside a poem inside a classroom inside a scary city called Beirut. The poem was by French surrealist Paul Éluard, and while listening to it for the first time, the little girl sitting at the left end of the first row, right there next to the stained glass window shielded by sandbags – meant to protect students from snipers and shrapnel – thought that there must be an earthquake hitting the country.

On my notebooks from school
On my desk and the trees
On the sand on the snow
I write your name

The teacher's voice was as gentle as ever, but for some reason it sounded like thunder. The little girl looked around her: no part of the ceiling had fallen; all the chairs and desks were in place; the books were in perfect order on the shelves; and her classmates were calm and focused. No earthquake then. Well, not outside, anyways.

On the glass of surprises
On lips that attend
High over the silence
I write your name

She could hardly notice that her heart was racing like a mad dog inside her chest, and that blood was rising to her feverish cheeks: nothing mattered; nothing existed but that magical flow of light and hope that was coming out from Miss Norma's larynx and into the little girl's life.

On my ravaged refuges
On my fallen lighthouses
On the walls of my boredom
I write your name

She wanted *that*, more of *that*, an endless amount of *that*; to receive *that*, but also to give it. At least, to try.

By the power of the word
I regain my life

Who said fertilisation processes can't be tracked accurately, even to the second? That was the exact moment the little girl knew she was going to be a writer.

This might come as a surprise to some, but the truth is many people in Lebanon and other Arab countries, women *and* men, think like I do. Feel like I do. Rage like I do. Or the other way around: I think and feel and rage like *them*. Some have the opportunity to express it, through literature and other forms of creativity or social activism. Others aren't that lucky. The latter are my point of leverage: their reactions to my texts are my version of fairy tales. They give me the power to get out of bed every morning, sit down at my desk, face the terrifying white screen, and bleed.

I owe all these anonymous women and men a great debt of gratitude. I keep on hearing their beautiful, hijacked voices echoing in my head, inspiring me and pushing me beyond my limits day after day, word after word. You deserve to hear them too. Thus I have decided, with their permission, to share a small number of them here with you. My intention is to show the variety of Arabs who rally around the same ideas, and to underline the fact that I am neither a 'lonely voice in the wilderness', nor an extraordinary exception. My 'microphone' simply works; theirs is broken. But one day it will be fixed. And oh how will they roar when that day finally comes.

Heba K. – Housewife – Palestinian:
I was married when I was sixteen, without being asked for my opinion, to a man who was twenty-one years older than me. He started beating me during the first week of our marriage. After three daughters and an infinite number of bruises all over my body, I decided to run away. With the help of a generous friend, I am now living in Berlin, and trying to stitch my soul up at the age of thirty-three. The only thing that I regret, the only thing that makes me ache, is to have been forced to leave my girls behind. I don't know if they will ever understand, or forgive me, but I had to go. My dignity couldn't afford it any more. It was either that, or killing myself. And I chose life. I hope that one day I will be strong and influential enough to save them as well. Us women have to stand up for ourselves and say no to violence before it is too late.

Fareed S. – Doctor – Egyptian:
I believe that we need to question what is happening around us, and decide for ourselves, instead of accepting being considered mindless herds. I resent that women are treated with such condescension in the Arab world. My daughter decided to wear the full veil when she became twenty-three, despite the fact that I urged, even begged, her not to. What could a father do in such a situation? I have raised her to be a secular free thinker, but society and her circle of friends have been stronger than me. I feel powerless, but I won't lose hope. I am sure that she will come back to her senses one day, and fight for her self-respect.

Wafaa B. – Nurse – Iraqi:
Since my early childhood, I was told repeatedly that I was good for nothing. At first, I was convinced of that as well. Until one day, I saw a documentary about Tamil women on TV. Particularly of Murugesapillai Koneswari, a Tamil mother of four, who challenged the authorities and filed an official complaint against police officers for stealing her property, despite the fear of retaliation. I thought: 'I need to start defending myself and believing in my potential.' So I went to a nursing school in secret, then I found a job at a local hospital in Basra. Now that I am bringing cash in, nobody in the family dares to stand in my way. Even my older brother, who used to mistreat me, has become passive, as he now asks me for money to buy alcohol and cigarettes. It is a small victory, but it is *my* victory, and I am proud of it.

Samir H. – Businessman – Lebanese:
I was born a Sunni and I have always felt that the people around me are tolerant and accommodating. These days I feel different. I almost feel threatened. Long beards everywhere. The number of veiled ladies exponentially increasing. Mosques are full on Fridays. I get phone calls every week from old friends asking me to

join their *tariqa* groups, or their charismatic sheikhs, or something as rotten. Not long ago these same friends were asking me to join them for drinks, parties or dinners. Some of them were even more liberal than me at some stage in their lives. That really worries me. I don't care what they do really, but I feel that the phenomenon is scary. I simply cannot stand injustice of any kind, in any form or under any disguise. Especially when such injustice is legalised by the Big Boss: Allah. I simply cannot take it and I cannot understand how people can still accept it. I must say I do not do anything about it; I gave up some time ago. The anger against injustice is there, but it stays inside me.

Amira G. – College student – Algerian:
I'm only twenty-two years old, and I am still a student, living in a very traditional and strict environment, but I aspire to become liberated one day. There are so many words inside of me that I would like to say but that I don't. Not yet, anyway. My road is long, but I have faith in my feet, and I know they will take me wherever I want to go.

Tahar M. – Pharmacist – Moroccan:
In these difficult times where the religious fascism and the patriarchal practices are growing increasingly in the Arab world, I believe that it is the power of women that we are missing, and that could save us from the abyss: brave women, rebel women, ready to denounce the hypocrisy of our societies, even at the cost of being attacked and threatened and hated. I guess I am a feminist. But then again, can I be that, being a man?

Amal B. – Secretary – Tunisian:
I am sick and tired of all the misogyny that surrounds me and tries to kill my spirit day after day. God is a mirage that has to do with our instinctive fear of death. Our biggest mistake is that

we made him up to cure that fear and save us from death by the illusion of the 'after death'. But the fantasy became bigger than us, and turned against us. The solution is to shoot the snake. Just kill it. Anything short of that is a waste of time. I am too weak and powerless to pull the trigger though.

Hussein T. – Lawyer – Syrian:
I am a fierce fighter for freedom of thought, and therefore against all forms of brainwashing, whether by religion, nationalism or cults of personality. Religion advocates differentiation between men: it puts believers against nonbelievers, one race against another race, males against females, etc. This needs to end. Soon.

Majed F. – Computer engineer – Yemeni:
Despite the fact that I am a man, and a fervent believer I should add, I refuse to be a macho. I come from a country where men and women are still strongly segregated. I have been raised to scorn all women, except my mother of course. While growing up, I never realised the absurdity of that inhumane education: we need to consecrate our mothers and treat them like saints, but treat all other women disrespectfully, including the mothers of our own children! Yet in my late thirties I have become conscious of this injustice, and I am trying to do something about it in the confines of my own home and small family. I can't take my ideas outside though: if I ever talk about such things with my friends, if I ever tell them that I believe women are equal to men, they make fun of me and tell me I am a sissy.

Eman S. – School teacher – Saudi:
I don't need to tell you what it means to be a Saudi woman: I assume you already know. I remember when I first read one of your books: I blushed although I was all alone in my room. It felt to me like I was committing the unthinkable, like I was

masturbating on top of *Jabal Arafat* on the tenth of *Du'l Hujjah*, with all the pilgrims watching. And when I heard footsteps on the stairs, I closed the book and jumped to exonerate myself from what I then thought was guilt. I don't think I understood you. But now I do. Now I want to be braver. But being brave here would cost me what I cannot afford.

Buthayna L. – Chemist – Kuwaiti:
Learning the Qur'an at an early age has handcuffed my freedom of expression. I learnt English in order to be able to say *sex* without lowering my gaze. To vocalise my needs, and not only to listen to those imposed by the man. Maybe one day I will muster enough courage to close all holy texts and celebrate my feelings and ideas in words both my soul and body know so well but are too God-ridden to express.

Nada K. – Sales person – Lebanese:
I was molested as a child by the same uncle who used to go to mass every Sunday. Now I am a mother of two girls, married to a man who has a golden cross hanging around his neck, and who rapes me repeatedly, but who I can't sue or divorce because the Lebanese law does not admit such a thing as 'marital rape'. Do you know what I wish for? That my girls will never be foolish enough to get married like me. I would love for them to be bigger than the white dress and solitaire ring and the mythological blessedness of sanctified matrimony. I would love for them to love with no fear, no boundaries. I would like to tell them that, and not feel like I am sabotaging them. Slowly, steadily, I am finding my tongue. It is still numb, and many layers of fear suffocate it. But I will find it somehow, someday.

At the beginning there was a word; a word that saved a little girl from suffocation; a word that saved her altogether; the same word that taught her to dream and to scream, in her head and on paper; the same word that is now tattooed in Arabic on the right arm of the woman she became; the same word that helps her stand up, every time she stumbles and falls to her knees; the same word that will be waiting for her, right there at the end of the journey, gleaming like a never-ending discovery. For like Éluard, and many others in her Arab world *and* on the face of this planet, that little girl is simply a human being who '*was born to know you / and to name you: / Freedom.*'

Letter to my sons

Stay hungry. Stay foolish.

Steve Jobs

My beloved,

Need I tell you that it has been the greatest, most enriching adventure of all being your mother these past twenty years? Well, it still is, and it will hopefully keep on being so for many years to come.

You have given me unconditional love, pride, consolation and strength, in moments of self-doubt, failure, disappointment and loneliness. You have been there for me, knowingly or unknowingly, at times when I haven't been able to be there for myself. You have embodied the light of hope in each dark tunnel I crossed, and my life jacket when drowning loomed. Yet I have a confession to make to you:

There are lots of things I did not tell you along the way: things I believed you would know instinctively. Things I thought you would grow up to find out on your own eventually. Things I assumed I could spare you the statement of. Things I decided I didn't want to preach to you, but to *illustrate* in front of you.

However, I have come to change my mind. I have come to think that some things need to be expressed clearly and directly, even at the cost of my words sounding like a dreary sermon or a hazardous generalisation. The fact that you are increasingly becoming adults (and about to explore the tricky mayhem of relationships) and my hope that you will rise to the challenge of being real men represent valid reasons for me to tell you some of those things, and this book is the perfect occasion to do so. So here they are:

We (women, most of us) are tired of you (men, most of you) seeing us as only your mothers, your daughters, your sisters, your lovers, your wives, your properties, your accessories, your servants, your toys …

We are tired of us not believing in ourselves. We are tired of you not believing in us. We are tired of us being evaluated as either not enough, or too much for you. We are tired of you assuming we all are commitment-freaks, and assuming yourselves to be commitment-phobics. We are tired of us feeling guilty because we are at work instead of home baking cookies. We are tired of you being persuaded we were made strictly to have babies, not to honour our dreams and careers just like you.

We are tired of us choosing the arseholes over the decent, the rough over the nice, and the rich and powerful over the ambitious and hard working. We are tired of you choosing the bitches over the honest, the fake over the genuine, and the young and beautiful over the loyal and loving (notwithstanding the fact we can be all of that concurrently). We are tired of us having to opt between manipulating you, and giving up on you. We are tired of you not letting yourselves go with our flow.

We are tired of us giving you our hand as an acknowledgement of compromise, instead of it being proof of intimacy and alliance. We are tired of you needing us to cover up with a black cloak or to overexpose ourselves like cheap sex objects in order for you to feel secure in your manhood. We are tired of us waiting for you to find us, instead of going out and finding you. We are tired of you deeming that needing us is a sign of weakness.

We are tired of us using the silent treatment with you. We are tired of you using the disdain treatment with us. We are tired of us not initiating sex for fear of being seen as pushy or labelled as aggressive. We are tired of you deciding what is 'ladylike' and what is not. We are tired of us worrying about the fat on our bellies, the depth of our cleavage and the make up on our faces. We are tired of you focusing on the fat on our bellies, the depth of our cleavage and the make up on our faces.

We are tired of us being labelled as romantic, and you as down-to-earth. We are tired of you running towards one-night stands as a detainee would run towards a barbed wire he doesn't know is electrified. We are tired of us imagining you are always up for sex. We are tired of you avoiding real heart-to-heart conversations. We are tired of us supposing we always 'get' you. We are tired of you supposing you can never understand us. We are tired of us confusing your chivalry with spinelessness. We are tired of you differentiating between sex and love. We are tired of us taking you as war trophies. We are tired of you taking us for granted.

We are tired of us faking orgasms to reassure you, keeping a low profile to support you, and telling you lies to cheer you up. We are tired of you feeling intimidated by our strength, threatened by our success, terrified by our intelligence, irritated by our freedom, challenged by our independence, and emasculated by our pride in being female. We are tired of us asking you for what is our due. We are tired of you not embracing us as equal partners.

We are tired of us thinking you are all made of ice. We are tired of you thinking we are all drama queens. We are tired of us being suspicious of you, compliant with you, or in combat against you.

We are tired of you denigrating us and our basic human rights in the name of Allah, traditions, physical supremacy, social dictates and the logic of 'who puts the bread on the table'.

We are tired of us having to prove to you that we are strong. We are tired of you having to prove to us that you are stronger. We are tired of us playing childish games in order to 'trap' you. We are tired of you obsessing about being seen as mere 'limp dicks' if you show us your vulnerable sides. We are tired of us not letting our real selves emerge in front of you. We are tired of you not approaching us and the world with a non-controlling, non-dominating mindset.

We are tired of us having impossible and unfair expectations from you. We are tired of you having an imbalanced blood distribution between your upper and lower body areas. We are tired of us blaming everything on our premenstrual syndrome. We are tired of you believing anything – even world hunger – can be solved by a Viagra tablet.

We are tired of us being prisoners of an alienating feminism. We are tired of you being prisoners of an alienating machismo.

Yes, we are unquestionably, utterly tired.
Now tell me: aren't you?

Happily ever after ...

Once upon a time, there was a little girl who hated Superman. She knew that only if *she* refuses to be a conciliating Scheherazade and/or a shallow Lois Lane, and only if *he* drops his mask and turns into a real Clark Kent for good, could they live 'happily' – that is, 'interestingly' – ever after.

So she used the only superpower she had in order to convince him, *and* herself:

Words.

THE END

Further reading

Recommended (and more 'serious') reads on the same inventions:

Eric Anderson, *The Monogamy Gap: Men, Love, and the Reality of Cheating*, New York, Oxford University Press, 2012.

Kathleen Lois Barry, *Unmaking War, Remaking Men: How Empathy Can Reshape Our Politics, Our Soldiers and Ourselves*, Santa Rosa, Phoenix Rising Press, 2011.

Simon Dermody, *The Lost Patriarch: Towards a New Mythology of Manhood*, Bloomington, AuthorHouse, 2007.

Charles Fourier, *The Hierarchies of Cuckoldry and Bankruptcy*, Cambridge, Mass., Wakefield Press, 2011.

David D. Gilmore, *Manhood in the Making: Cultural Concepts of Masculinity*, New Haven, Yale University Press, 2003.

E.J. Graff, *What is Marriage for?*, Boston, Beacon, 1999.

Christopher Hitchens, *God is Not Great: How Religion Poisons Everything*, New York, Warner Twelve, 2007.

Mara Hvistendahl, *Unnatural Selection: Choosing Boys over Girls, and the Consequences of a World Full of Men*, New York, PublicAffairs, 2011.

Laura Kipnis, *Against Love: A Polemic*, New York, Pantheon, 2003.

Gerda Lerner, *The Creation of Patriarchy*, New York, Oxford University Press, 1986.

Bill Lauritzen, *The Invention of God: The Natural Origins of Mythology and Religion*, StreetWrite, 2011.

Susan Squire, *I Don't: A Contrarian History of Marriage*, New York, Bloomsbury, 2008.

Elizabeth Wurtzel, *Bitch: In Praise of Difficult Women*, New York, Doubleday, 1998.

Acknowledgements

This book is a true 'citizen' of the world. It has been written on the road, respectively in Rome, Berlin, Marseilles, Cartagena, Milan, Brussels, Madrid, Naples, Genoa, Miami, Toronto, Copenhagen, Toulouse, Paris, London, Malmö, Ann Arbor, Oslo, Segovia, Algiers, New York, Washington, Boston, Olinda, Rio de Janeiro, Stockholm, Amsterdam, The Hague, Providence, Narvik and Beirut. So I would like to begin by thanking the airports and hotels of the above cities for having tolerated: firstly, my frantic search for power outlets to recharge my laptop battery and secondly, my frequent complaints about noisy neighbours interfering with my flow of thoughts. Special thanks go to Hossein, the Iranian taxi driver in the Norwegian capital, whose simple words about secularism, womens rights and manhood inspired me one winter morning more than many books written by experts about the same subjects. I had promised Hossein at the time that he'd find himself in my next book: promise fulfilled.

Secondly, I offer my sincerest gratitude to the fantastic friends who took the time to read my gibberish, and gave me perceptive, valuable comments on making a decent book out of it. These are (in alphabetical order): Hatem Badih, Silio Boccanera, Tod Brilliant, Peter Carlsson, David Demarest, Hala Habib, Schona Jolly, Michael Moore, Salvatore Pitruzzello, Mona Rahhal, Tony Saade, Zeina Nader Salwan, Jan Henrik Swahn and Abir Ward.

I also thank all the men that I have met in my life. All of them, indeed: the good, the bad and the ugly. They have made me grow, each in his own way: with the embraces they gave me as much as the scars they left on me; with the smiles they provoked on my face as much as the disappointments they caused in my heart; with the conversations they stirred between us as much as the loneliness they deepened around me. It goes without saying that listing their names here won't do anybody any good. But let them know I couldn't have done it without them.

In addition, I would like to thank the two special men I grew up with: my father, Atallah, and my brother, Chadi. They have both, each in his own way, strengthened my trust in the potential of manhood to evolve.

A big thank you is due to my precious, faithful readers all over the world: for the letters and emails they send me, for the hugs they give me, and most of all for their miraculous faith in me. I don't know where I would have been today without their constant encouragement and support.

Last but not least, I would like to thank my loved ones for putting up with my mood swings and my scandalous disregard for their needs while I am writing. I know for a fact that I can be a selfish bitch when I am in 'creative mode'. So here is the perfect opportunity to say sorry to:

My eldest son, Mounir, for often nodding at his words without really listening to what he was saying. I sure hope I haven't accidentally nodded at 'Mom, can I take drugs and get wasted?'

My youngest son, Ounsi, for not kissing him as often as I should, and wanted to. And for taking advantage of his great massage techniques whenever my neck was killing me from too many hours sitting down.

My mother, Mary, for gratuitously shouting at her every time she tried to put food into my mouth while I was on the computer, and on other occasions as well, where she showed nothing but unconditional generosity and care. It is never too late to feel ashamed of one's ungratefulness.

My beloved Marianne for not having told her every second

how beautiful she looked with her magnificent pregnant belly; or how very lucky I am to have her in my life.

And finally, allow me to humbly thank the fire of passion (some call it 'madness') that I was born/blessed with. It is the source of my fighting spirit, the one that has motivated me, guided me and empowered me to take on this, and other challenges; the one that has made and still makes me despise the injustices and the inhumanities that I witness; the one that has allowed and still allows me to endure the outrage of my critics and the condemnation of the Neanderthals around me. That spirit has contributed immensely to this book, and to my each and every endeavour in life. I am quite certain I wouldn't get out of bed in the morning without it ... Why would I? A good warrior knows that identifying the foe is never enough:

She knows she is useless without her flaming arrows.[2]

---

2   You are welcome to contact the author and share your comments, stories and experiences with her: Email: contact@joumanahaddad.com Twitter: @joumana333 Facebook: http://facebook.com/joumanajo.haddad